P

)))) ((((

From publishers who wouldn't publish

The Man on the Grassy Knoll

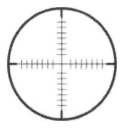

Crown Books – "The writing here is pretty engaging . . ."

Harper - ". . . backstory is fascinating… the narrative here feels like the straightforward musings of a real person as opposed to a piece of fiction. It is entirely understandable why you would read this manuscript and wonder if it were an actual, credible document."

Little, Brown – "There's much to like here."

NAL – "This book has much to recommend it…"

Putnam – "It's very clever… nice style. …very clever stuff."

———

Ron Wiggins, columnist, author – "It made my hair stand up. . . there's no doubt in my mind what really happened in Dallas."

The Man on the Grassy Knoll

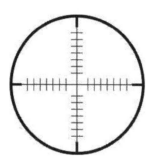

Foreword by George Williams

Cover design by George Williams
with Bryce Adkins
Cover Photo taken by Mary Moorman

The Man on the Grassy Knoll

Anonymous

Grey Knight Press
Palm Beach, FL

The Man on the Grassy Knoll

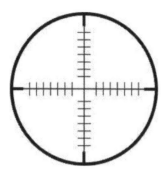

ISBN-13 # 978-0615531557   ISBN-10# 0615531555
Library of Congress catalog # applied for

Foreword

I write movies and the occasional failed novel. When this journal was optioned for theatrical production, I was tasked with developing a screenplay from the narrative. I had known nothing about the work or its history, only that the author was hidden behind a legal veil. The manuscript had been copyrighted anonymously through the Miami law firm of Akerman Senterfitt, which apparently did not know the identity of its client, having been paid for its services in cash.

Every American born before 1990 knows where he or she was on the morning of September 11, 2001. For those of us who entered this life before 1950, there is one other day seared in our memory, an afternoon when we all know where we were and what we were doing: November 22, 1963. I had graduated college in June of that year, five months before the assassination of President John F. Kennedy in Dallas. The tragic and powerful emotions we shared, our collective national consciousness and common experience as witness to the unfolding tragedy of that weekend, marked a singular event in human history brought about by the immediacy and ubiquitous nature of television.

This anonymous work came with quite a history. I was at once interested, skeptical and curious. **Sixty Minutes** had investigated the journal, as had various Kennedy

The Man on the Grassy Knoll

assassination experts from forensic pathologists to historians to attorneys involved in the event or its aftermath. The general consensus was that the narrative presented a more likely version of the events in Dallas than the Warren Commission report, although few would go on the record and say so.

I was unprepared for the emotional impact of the journal. Contributing to this was the fact that the protagonist, in a curious coincidence, also graduated college in 1963. I was able to readily identify firsthand with much of what he wrote.

Whether true or not, **The Man on the Grassy Knoll** has the unmistakable air of authenticity. I found myself chilled by the almost clinical, journalistic presentation, the ordinary details to these extraordinary events, the terrible insight into the mind of Lee Harvey Oswald. I was swept along by the understated emotional currents to this tidal wave of American history. The adaptation of this work to the screen has proven an emotional and challenging experience.

What are you about to read? I leave it to the reader to decide.

George Williams
Palm Beach, Florida
August, 2011

Prologue

My name - real or otherwise - has never appeared on the payroll of the Central Intelligence Agency or any of the other clandestine services. There were no pay stubs, no W-2's or 1099's. Payment was via wire transfer to an offshore Bahamian account. Only a handful of agency personnel was ever aware of my existence, or the operation for which I was recruited; even less knew the actual mission I carried out in November, 1963 as a contract worker. This cadre is probably all dead. I never met my counterpart, AM/LASH, or any of the other government-paid assassins associated with Project Rifle, although in recent years his code name has surfaced on a number of documents, released through the Freedom of Information Act. As far as I know, there is no document at all with my name on it, and likely never was, except the Authorization to Release Information form and Secrecy Agreement I signed my senior year in college. These papers were deliberately destroyed in December 1963 or early 1964.

Several years passed between the events of 1963 and re-contact with the person who directed my actions in that year. It was only then that the remaining pieces to the puzzle fell into place and formed a ghastly picture of the only successful coup d'état in American history: the assassination of the President of the United States by agents of his own

The Man on the Grassy Knoll

government, thereby removing him and his brother from office and altering the course of clandestine warfare against another sovereign state. This is part of that story.

Introduction

Publication of this journal has probably been triggered by my death. I don't think you will weep for me.

I wrote this alone – I had no choice – and the name you see as author is not real. While the duty to history is great, and this document must see the light of day, I must protect those loved ones around me from the knowledge of my participation in one of history's blackest events. There is no member of my family, no friend, no acquaintance, no other person of any description with an inkling of my involvement in the assassination of a President of the United States. As far as I ever knew, knowledge of my actions extended to a Mr. Smith, whomever he worked with, or for, Lee Oswald, and a certain remarkable priest in Arizona. As for the latter, he carried the heaviest burden in silence for decades, bound by the tenets of the Roman Catholic Church. For these reasons my anonymity must remain preserved, even if I have not survived.

A second occurrence may activate release of this work: inquiries about a safety deposit box containing one Soviet military firearm, several rounds of special ammunition, two drinking glasses, a Texas license plate number and identification for a fictitious person, written on an airline ticket envelope, and a rifle serial number. The likelihood of this happening is small.

Sometime around February, 1964, I forced myself to recall all that occurred since the spring of 1963. To start with, I possessed one detailed four page document, transcribed by me immediately following a September meeting in a Chinese restaurant in Phoenix. I made extensive notes on conversations, dates, places and times. Handwritten on yellow legal paper, they numbered close to thirty pages. These lay undisturbed for several months. It was only then that I could sit down and truly attempt to reconstruct, in narrative form, those fateful days. It proved a wrenching experience. I had hoped the project would yield answers, some measure of clarity, a degree of understanding; it did none of these.

Most of what you will read, then, was written in late 1964. There was then another long hiatus. The events of 1963 have assumed a dreamlike quality, almost as though reading about someone else in a once-familiar novel. Certain details are as yesterday, and others, in truth, I remember not at all. Mr. Smith's shirts, for instance. Expensive and tailored, not at all like a government employee, I see them as well as I can recall the essence of his odd, but pleasant, cologne. For the business he was in, he was somewhat of a dandy, and the contrast was not easily forgotten. The most vivid memory, misted in red, is the split-second view through my rifle scope of the results of my participation. This memory, unfortunately, does not diminish. It flashes before me still, without warning, staining the corners of the room, and it will never stop.

I believe I can say that reconstruction beyond memory or notes is limited to the odd preposition, adjective, or other necessary grammatical glue. The quilt may be patchy, but the threads are real. The conversations are, I think, remarkably intact. Dates and sequence, I must confess, have been less reliable but the 1964 notes were extensive. Without them, I could not recall what happened where, in which month and what order. There may still be errors, but I have done the best I could.

I believe the reader may be disappointed in the reality. So much has been written, filmed, discussed, analyzed, made into myth that it is inevitable the truth, while still more grotesque than fiction, will leave a sense of want. The assassination of an American president, especially one whose legacy is now cloaked in a legendary raiment, was a great turning point downward in this nation's history. The stuff of the event itself, so long shrouded in mystery, secrecy and controversy, would seem to need a higher purpose, a misguided but ennobling raison d'être, a plan of vast scope and complexity, and, finally answers which I can only partially provide. I can only relate in a personal sense uncertainty, monetary avarice, and stumbling inevitability, all tinged with the purple of tragic confusion. For Lee Harvey Oswald, I can only offer the reality of his meanness, his commonness, his *smallness*, which all seems so incomprehensible against the backdrop of his sixth floor window. I cannot apologize for this but I do recognize it. I report it faithfully with no purpose other than to tell the truth.

Frankly, the work leaves me with some disappointment. I tried to set everything down in a journalistic way, but, of course, personal style shades the manuscript. Even in those years immediately following the assassination,

The Man on the Grassy Knoll

when the pursuit of redemption and its hopeless acquisition were my essence, I detect in the writing a muted defiance, a hint of excuse, an unintended naiveté, an attempt to win over the reader to the point of view that I was just a young, all-American, inexperienced student manipulated to evil ends by a shadowy intelligence community. If I had written this today, I would hope these characteristics would not color the writing.

I trust the demarcations of the narrative are understandable. A few names and locations have been changed, but only to preserve my anonymity. It would be, for instance, very easy to trace my identity with the knowledge of a specific hotel in a particular college town, where I first met Mr. Smith. The pitching staff of the Class of 1963 consisted of only a handful of young hurlers. All other locations are real.

I have largely resisted the temptation to revise the original manuscript (Part I) with material learned much later, for several reasons, perhaps the most important being historical accuracy, and to avoid the more balanced perspective of time. There have been a few modifications to the first chapters, primarily to explain the circumstances that existed in 1963, for those unfamiliar with that era.

*   *   *   *   *   *

After more than half a lifetime of silence, then, I speak. In truth, I cannot hope to purge myself of the responsibility for the enormity of my participation; I am resigned to the realization that my life has been forever shadowed by those careless days.

Part I

1963

The Man on the Grassy Knoll

Chapter 1

It was the spring of my senior year in college, and I was looking forward to graduation and a promising future, albeit with little idea what that future might be. Pitching for the varsity baseball team, I was enjoying my best year with an ERA of 2.40. Any year was a good year when my GPA was higher than my Earned Run Average. My grade point for the fall term had been about a 3.1. The job market seemed promising, the economy was rolling along, and I was trying to decide between law school and taking a job. The corporate recruiters were interviewing me and my classmates, and attractive offers were beginning to materialize for the Class of 1963. Not for me, though.

During this time there was a great pressure to conform to society's stereotypical college graduate. For most of us, the idea of working for a large company, usually in a management training program, was the normal progression from university life. There was a natural order, and not many thought to question it. I certainly hadn't, at least until the recruiters began showing up on campus. The problem was that I was having difficulty relating to any of my interviews. We had attended workshops given by the Placement Office as to the correct manner of being interviewed. These were hard to take seriously. We were instructed how to dress, how to sit, respond to questions, and the like. Many of us had to buy our first adult suit. Our introduction to corporate life made it seem almost like military service. My discomfort was acute. Clearly, I was not going to do well without a great deal of effort and self-control I was not sure I possessed.

I found I had little interest in working for any of these companies. I was going through the motions, primarily because I did not know what else to do. I am sure this surfaced as less than an enthusiastic demeanor during the few interviews I scheduled. All the recruiters seemed polished and self-assured, and possessed of a certainty about things I did not have. They had a way of making me feel as if many of life's secrets were eluding me. I detected a faint disdain for Liberal Arts majors. During one interview with a major tire and rubber company, the recruiter asked me what my real interest in rubber was. The absurdity of this question took me aback. I don't exactly remember my answer but it was truthful. As a result, I was going to graduate with no job unless I really bucked up. I was getting discouraged.

I'd been fortunate, landing a partial free ride for baseball. My dad worked hard, but I don't know if he could have afforded an expensive school like mine without financial assistance. I was glad to be able to contribute. As a starter in the regular rotation, I was completing my third varsity year, each with a winning record, striking out just over thirteen batters per game. My batting average was .320. With those numbers, I was hoping to be recruited by professional baseball. This was one reason I had no firm future plans. Our pitching coach, a former major leaguer, hadn't the slightest idea how to teach, but told endless funny stories about his adventures in the big leagues. His tales kept me motivated; I knew I would have no trouble adjusting to life in the majors. He constantly told me I had the stuff to make it if I could improve my curve ball.

As a freshman athlete, I'd been assigned to the athletic dorm. After a few days I realized that wasn't really a good idea. The football players blocked and tackled each other constantly, splintering doors and breaking furniture. The hockey players shot pucks down the halls, whacking their sticks off the linoleum and sending the lethal disks crashing into walls, doors, and ceilings, shattering fire alarms and light bulbs behind protective wire cages, exploding showers of plaster and ceiling tile everywhere. The A dorm was also a magnet for freshman girls, who, I quickly learned, were snuck in routinely.

An interesting place, if not very conducive to good study habits.

*　　　　*　　　　*

Someone gets caught in traffic, misses a flight: lives change. A casual glance at a crowded party: eyes meet, destinies alter. Inconsequential actions, small decisions. The beat of butterfly wings.

Freshman roommates are assigned, and the future of a country changes.

Ramon Figueroa was tall and rangy, a southpaw pitcher also on scholarship. Like his countrymen, he'd played baseball since he could first toddle onto the ragged, stony diamond not far from his home in Playa Giron, on the south coast of Cuba. My roommate had the gift of storytelling, and at night he'd tell me of the beautiful sandy beaches of Playa

Giron, the rustling palms, and the canopy of stars above the rocky, infertile soil that stretched across the countryside to green mountains rising into heavy, moisture-laden clouds. As he spoke, I heard salsa music punctuated by the laughter of musky Cuban women; I listened to the hissing surf as emerald water slid up the white, wide beaches toward the shrugging palms yards from his home. I tasted black beans and rice, the sweet flavor of the plantain, and savory, juicy pork through his words as we lay in the darkness. Breathing deeply, I inhaled the sweet flowery aroma of the El Ray del Mundo, the pungent aroma of café con leche. I leaned on my pillow and heard the click of dominoes palmed by the old men sitting outside their ramshackle dwellings, laughing and smoking and telling stories of baseball and fishing and toiling in the tropical haze of the day. I saw them sitting after their supper of arroz con pollo y frijoles negro, shrouded in the blue smoke of the evening, cigar tips lighting the night like fireflies, darting this way and that with their expansive gestures. Ramon's grandfather Ernesto had been a reader in the great cigar halls of Havana, perhaps the highest position of honor in his trade, sitting on a dais intoning the works of the great Castilian writers of Catalan. Ernesto brought their words to life in a booming, authoritative voice as the workers crafted their fine cigars, made with the leaves grown on the slopes of mountains soaked in the rain and heat of that tropical island.

Ramon had his grandfather's gift, as you can probably tell, because those were pretty much his words. I had known little about Cuba, and nothing at all about cigar making or Cuban food, but I felt the tug of that tropical, exotic land through my roommate's storytelling. Besides being a craftsman with language, Ramon had a ninety mph fastball, pinpoint control and a wicked curve. He was also a power hitter with a .350 average. No question, the kid had a future.

Ramon had been stateside less than a year, and told me his father had seen the blood on the wall when the rebels took Santa Clara around New Year's Day in 1959. His family had money, and the Figueroas had managed to leave Cuba with a little of it. They settled in Miami, a century away, as he put it, from Playa Giron. Ramon loved America; he loved almost everything about his newly adopted country. He loved television and Elvis and the Yankees and General Motors, especially the Cadillac El Dorado, and he still had enough left over to love Cuba and Playa Giron. We communicated in a kind of Spanglish for awhile. Each improved rapidly because of the other. We became fast friends, pledging the same fraternity.

When Ramon learned I was a target shooter, he expressed an interest in coming with me to the local firing range, where I had joined the shooting club. I was glad for the company. We visited the range once or twice a month, and he proved a pretty fair marksman. He obviously had been around weapons. I asked him about his prior experience, and he shrugged.

"I used to shoot my dad's Mousqueton," he said. I had never seen the French carbine, but I knew it was held in high regard. He'd killed a dangerous salt water crocodile and several of the obnoxious hutia, an omnivorous rodent that grew to two feet in length. I'd never heard of the hutia, and hoped we didn't have them in the U.S.

During the freshman baseball season, Ramon's family came up to see him pitch. His father Abelardo was a burly, beefy guy with a thin moustache whose muscles strained the pure white guayabera he wore. His mother Ramira, barely five feet tall, spoke little but had quick, darting intelligent eyes. Somehow she looked as though she had just come out of the kitchen. Marisol was just a year younger than Ramon, sultry and beautiful, with dark, wavy hair and a penetrating gaze that seemed to fix on me from the stands as I sat in the bullpen. Ramon honored his family that day with a two hit shutout and a double into the right field corner, driving in the winning run. Marisol jumped and clapped, as did her father, and I could hear his booming voice from my chair in right field.

After the game, we all went to dinner in town. Ramon had to help his dad with the menu; it was apparently the first time in Abelardo Figueroa's life he couldn't order *arroz con pollo*. I sat across from Mirasol, and found she shared her brother's gift. She told me of their childhood, swimming in the transparent waters off Playa Giron, floating over coral heads and swaying fans. There were funny stories about Ramon as a boy, which would have embarrassed him if he hadn't been engrossed in conversation with his father. She described the culture shock she'd experienced moving to Miami, all the funny little differences, and had been surprised how many other Cuban girls attended her high school. Like her brother, she embraced America, especially Moon Pies and RC Cola, hot dogs and cheeseburgers. She loved Tito Puente and Jerry Lee Lewis.

Mirasol was very interested in my background. She asked about my family life, and wondered how I was enjoying living away from home. I told her, truthfully, that one of the best things about school was having Ramon for a roommate. She asked me what I thought about Cuba, and Fidel, and even Che Guevara, who I knew from Ramon's informal history

6

lessons was Fidel's revolutionary buddy. The evening passed, it seemed, in just a few minutes. When they were leaving, I asked her a question.

"Are you coming for another visit this year?" I saw Ramira's eyebrow arch. I guess she was a wily one, or maybe I wasn't too good at acting very suavely. Probably I wasn't too good at acting suavely.

Mirasol smiled. "I hope so." Mama's eyes flicked between us. Her face was expressionless. "I'd like to see you pitch as well," Mirasol added.

My heart jumped. I know how that sounds, but it did anyway. The season had maybe another six weeks to go. I really looked forward to the possibility of seeing Marisol in that time, but she didn't make it. She knew my address, of course, as it was the same as her brother's, and wrote me two weeks after returning to Miami. I didn't mention it to Ramon. We corresponded for the rest of the year and grew close. I'd never even held her hand or kissed her, but I kind of felt as though I had.

The next time we saw each other was in March, 1961, just about a year later. Mirasol was now a college freshman. She came up with her dad for a weekend and saw Ramon pitch again, but they didn't stay long enough for my next scheduled start. Mirasol and I managed a few moments alone, after the game. Ramon and Abelardo were huddled under a tree, in some intense conversation, and so we slipped away. We walked up a footpath between elms and stands of birch behind fraternity row, squirrels darting up their trunks as we passed. We kissed and embraced; she reached up and twirled my hair, laughing, and said *mi novio*. She told me her mother found me amusing, and a nice guy for a gringo. The way she said it, it seemed a pretty big compliment. I could tell her mother's approval was very important to her. Mirasol said she would try and come up again from school before the year ended.

But she didn't. A couple of days later, as I was heading off to class, Ramon called to me from his desk. I turned in the doorway of our room, on the top floor of the fraternity house.

"If something happens to me," he said, "I want you to take care of my sister."

"What?" The remark had come from left field. "What the hell are you talking about?"

"Please, John. Promise me. I know what she thinks of you."

I didn't know what to think, but I promised him I would. It seemed he knew about me and Mirasol, although there really wasn't much to tell. He'd never said a word. Maybe she told him we had written each other. I mulled over my roommates words as I walked to class, feeling a chill that wasn't just the morning crispness.

Two days later, in the middle of baseball season, in the middle of the semester, Ramon disappeared. Just like that. All his stuff was gone when I came back from English Lit class. I checked with our coach and the school authorities; they were as puzzled as I. Miami information showed a zillion Figueroas in that city but the only number for A. Figueroa was unlisted.

Ramon never set foot on campus again. I tried calling Mirasol at college but couldn't reach her. I left messages and wrote her straightaway but received no answer. I was left bewildered, with a great sense of loss, wondering what the hell was going on. It would be more than three years before I knew.

8

Chapter 2

Ramon might have been able to knock off a two foot hutia, but I could shoot the eyes out of a six inch rodent when I was eleven years old. My Remington 572 FieldMaster .22 and I made rats an endangered species at our local dump. Even the small, quick field mice stood no chance against my pump action rimfire rifle; I could squeeze off two rounds per second with accuracy. Our family had a tradition of bearing arms, and I'd been thrilled on my eleventh birthday to get the Remington. We had room to practice and often did, plinking targets, vermin and beer cans. My friends and I competed with each other, holding informal shooting contests at the landfill. We probably ventilated about a hundred refrigerators, ovens, and a zillion beer cans during high school. Road signs were fair game from moving cars. We never missed a deer season and usually brought home a buck.

Over my collegiate four years, I got to know a number of regulars from the shooting club. Many were excellent marksmen. There were local competitions and occasionally I participated. The town newspaper sometimes published the results of regional matches. My name appeared a few times when I did well. The cost of ammunition was a consideration for a student and as a result I did not practice or compete as often as I might have liked.

9

The Man on the Grassy Knoll

Early in my senior year, I acquired the semi-automatic F N FAL rifle, known in the U.S. as the T48. The weapon was almost new and got my attention because it was underpriced. Manufactured in America by H&R, this was not a common rifle in the United States. The FAL was used by NATO troops. Empty, the weapon weighed a little over eight pounds, which felt about right for me. Guns are very personal choices. I had experience with one other F N Belgian rifle and liked it. Their weapons seemed accurate and well-made. The only drawback was that the FAL was designed to use the fully powered 7.62mm NATO cartridge, which wasn't cheap. Recoil was heavy and thus the weapon did not lend itself to rapid fire. Students could not keep arms on campus, and the rifle club was an on-again off-again type of thing, and so I stored the T48 in a lockup facility a couple of blocks off school grounds.

I used that rifle often, on the range and elsewhere, and really felt at home with the gun. I became very accurate with it; the scope mounted on the T48 was of good quality and thus the rifle became a formidable weapon. I entered the NRA sectional competition and was lucky enough to win. As a result, I qualified for the nationals, scheduled for later in the year. The campus rag printed a flattering article, and I got a few lines in the local newspaper.

On a Sunday afternoon in March 1963, an unusual event occurred that would eventually have unimaginable repercussions. Three of us – David Hendrick, Marshall Polk and myself, all seniors and target shooters - had driven several miles out of town to a wooded area that backed up to a landfill. While not officially sanctioned, many locals used the area for recreational shooting as the hill behind formed a natural backstop for firing. No one complained and the cops didn't care. We'd been there several times over the past two years. I knew I was going to need a lot more practice to do well at the national level.

It was around 2 p.m. when we arrived. The sky was clear, quite bright, with winds gusting to maybe 20 mph. It was an invigorating spring afternoon. I loaded my weapon while Hendrick set empty soda cans atop a striped traffic horse left there for just that purpose. I don't recall exactly where Polk was or what he was doing when it happened.

A gust of wind blew over an empty can and David bent down to reset it atop the wooden barrier. As he did, something careened around the hill, incredibly fast, and made straight for my classmate. For a split second, I didn't recognize the dark shape. It was within yards of Hendrick when I raised the T48 as fast as I could and fired. The bear dropped immediately; it had been charging so swiftly it actually tumbled to a stop and crashed into David's leg. He stood frozen for a moment, mouth ajar, before leaping back with a holler and running a couple of steps away. When we cautiously approached, it was obvious the creature was dead. I'd drilled him in the chest and again in the throat, tearing his heart and killing him instantly.

It turned out this black bear had created a dangerous situation for nearby residents over the past month, raiding garbage cans and ripping garments off clotheslines. The animal had eluded attempts at capture. The paper ran the story on page one, with photos of us and the bear, and made a big deal out of my "lighting reactions and amazing marksmanship". The reporter wrote the bear weighed 350 pounds, which seemed to me about 150 pounds too much, but it made a good story. I guess it was a slow news day. The truth was, I wasn't that far away, and I was somewhat lucky. Polk told the guy I'd only fired twice, but I'd actually gotten off three rounds. He figured the readers didn't need to know I missed once. Kendrick gushed how I was the NRA national high powered rifle champion and that I'd saved his life. I tried to correct my classmate, but the reporter just thought I was being modest, I suppose, or maybe he didn't care, because he printed it anyway. If that wasn't embarrassing enough, the local network station came out and did a piece on me, showing stock footage of some giant grizzly. It must have been broadcast regionally, because even my mom saw it. I thought the stupid story would never end; pretty soon they'd show me knocking off King Kong. I even got a call from the local taxidermist, asking if I wanted the bear mounted. I considered the idea until I found out what it cost. Later, of course, Polk and Kendrick made me buy them a case of beer apiece. Those guys laughed and joked for weeks about the whole thing.

Someone else had seen the story too, as I would learn. Someone with more than a casual interest.

Someone who wasn't laughing or joking.

*   *   *   *

I enjoyed my four years of college life. It may be surprising to the reader, considering the subject matter of this journal, but things were pretty normal and mainstream for me. Going to the range provided an excellent outlet from the rigors of studying and the collegiate grind. Shooting was relaxing, and I enjoyed improving my marksmanship. I also liked the movies, parties, sports and all the usual campus recreational activities. Riflery had its place, but was not a dominant activity. I was a member of a popular fraternity, dated often and had two or three girlfriends during that time. None evolved into a very serious relationship. For awhile, after Mirasol disappeared along with her brother, I kept company with a woman a few years older than me who taught second grade in town. Linda was tall and slender, almost ethereal, with a smile that made you feel as though you shared a special secret. She had an apartment within walking distance and we had a fulfilling relationship, especially since she liked to cook. Her liver with onions and bacon was wonderful, even tastier than my mom's.

Could life have been better?

Back then, I would never have even thought to ask.

Chapter 3

There were various political organizations at school. Young Republicans, Democrats, and several other groups were active on campus. I had few political convictions and no interest in these clubs. If anything, I would have described myself as a lukewarm Republican.

There were fringe groups as well. In those days, it was dangerous to flirt with Communism. The atmosphere was thick with the threat of Soviet might, and the Cuban missile crisis had heated the Cold War near the flash point. Nonetheless, it was common knowledge that some kind of Socialist or Communist student organization existed on campus. This clandestine group was rumored to meet monthly. I knew no one who admitted to being a member. I cannot recall, but our school may also have had a chapter of the John Birch Society. There was something for everyone.

In April of my senior year, several of us heard this Marxist cell was going to meet in the backroom of a local tavern, the Copper Tankard, during the coming week. There were maybe a half dozen of us hanging around the fraternity main room when the subject came up. Dale Elliot, another senior, suggested that a couple of us attend. The rest of us looked at him strangely.

"What else is there to do on a Wednesday night?" he asked.

"Study for finals?" I volunteered. Everyone ignored me. Exams were still weeks off.

"I bet they've got free vodka," somebody said. The three or four others in the room laughed. That was enough for Jeffrey Spears, a marketing major.

"Hell, I'll go even if it's just beer."

Jeffrey and Dale worked on the rest of us. Someone suggested that I go along, since they all knew I was not having a great deal of success with my employment interviews. Maybe I could get a job working for the Communists. Someone else said they would probably be the only people who would hire me.

"Hey, maybe you could pitch for the Cincinnati Reds," Jeff said. "Get it?" That got a chuckle out of everyone.

I sighed. Actually, the idea was no worse than many others over the past four years. We'd spent many nights pursuing equally stupid ends. When I thought about it, some were definitely more inane. A few were illegal. It was college, wasn't it?

I recalled the vision of Nikita Khrushchev pounding the U.N. table with his shoe a couple of years earlier. The idea of little guys looking like Lenin or Marx in ill-fitting wool suits, sitting around some dingy table smoking acrid foreign cigarettes, drinking vodka and singing the Song of the Volga Boatmen struck me as funny. Anyway, there probably were no students on campus fitting that description.

I said I'd tag along.

Without a great deal of thought, then, and with nothing in mind but a little entertainment, three of us decided to attend. It was as ordinary, as bizarre, as a thousand other things. I gave the matter little thought until Wednesday evening. Jeff banged on my room door about 7:30 with Dale in tow. I was surprised either remembered, but there they were.

Their appearance was a welcome break from studying. We walked the short distance off campus on a clear and soft evening. The tavern was not far; across two streets and the lighted COPPER TANKARD sign came into view.

We did not know whether the organization would view prospective new members with open arms or suspicion. Maybe they wouldn't even allow us in. As we approached the bar, I wondered what sort of nuts belonged to this club. Were they foreign exchange students? The lunatic fringe? Book nerds from the library secretly planning to blow up the fraternities? Then again, did I really care?

The bars and taverns in town catered either to blue collar working people or students. The town-gown situation was clearly delineated. There were a few ethnic clubs, such as the German-American Club and the Italian-American Club, but as far as I knew these were not frequented by my classmates, except maybe on Columbus Day or during a Bavarian beer festival. This particular tavern in question was a campus hangout.

We entered the place around 8 p.m., the meeting time according to our sources. The decor was sparse, with sawdust and peanut shells on the wood floor. The bar itself was along the left wall, and fairly well-lit. Across the dance floor were a series of booths, perhaps eight or ten, and a curtained doorway connected to the back poolroom. When we entered, there were about a dozen people in the main room. They were all guys, so no one was dancing. I don't think there was any music, anyway. We strolled through the curtain and into the poolroom.

The Man on the Grassy Knoll

The pool table surface was covered with a plywood sheet, it appeared, and an old, stained white tablecloth lay atop the surface. There were perhaps eight or nine young adults milling about, engaged in a number of conversations. A couple of these were female, and believe me they were not knockouts. I could see why they might be mad at society. Folding chairs had been placed around the table itself but they were as yet unoccupied. As we approached the pool area, the talk dwindled and finally stopped altogether. I looked over the group and did not recognize any of the people in the room. Some did not appear to be students.

A tall young man with an engaging smile stepped toward us. He wore a checkered shirt and had a bandage on one hand.

"Can we help you?" he asked.

"Maybe," Jeffrey said. "We're looking for a meeting."

The young man tilted his head quizzically. "What kind of meeting are you looking for?"

"One that didn't appear on the bulletin board," Jeffrey continued.

"How did you hear about it?" he asked.

"Everybody knows about your group. Do you think it's a big secret or something?"

This seemed to surprise Checkered Shirt.

"We think we can help but we don't know how," Jeff continued, softening his tone. I was finding a new respect for my fraternity brother. I hadn't known he could be that smooth. Then again, he was a marketing major.

The Man on the Grassy Knoll

Another group member spoke up. "What are you talking about? You're going to have to be more specific," he asked.

"We're unhappy with what happened in Cuba. We don't agree with the way our government is operating. Maybe we're looking for a better way."

Spears was on a roll. I suppressed a laugh. This was only done on a lark, a moment's careless thought, and now my friend was getting us into God-knows-what. What an actor, though.

Checkered Shirt spoke. "Fine. Glad to have you." He stuck out his hand, the unbandaged one. We all shook hands and made brief introductions. I didn't hear half their names or remember any of them except the spokesman. He was David. He said, "We need to see your student I.D. cards."

Now this was an uncomfortable surprise. I was uneasy about having our identities revealed, particularly since we'd only been given their first names. Jeffrey and Dale took out their I.D. cards - actually Student Health Service cards - and handed them over to one of the Bolsheviks. I hesitated for a moment, and then withdrew mine from my wallet. In for a penny, in for a pound. I shrugged and handed it over.

On such small things can the course of history change.

The cards were briefly examined and handed to someone behind the pool table. To my dismay, this individual sat down and copied our names onto a yellow sheet. In a few moments, we had our cards back.

"Sit down and join us. The meeting is about to start." So that was it. No questions, no grilling, no suspicion. How easy it would be, I thought, if we were government spies. Some Communists.

The Man on the Grassy Knoll

What I recall about the meeting itself is hazy. They discussed, passionately, the 1961 "invasion" of Cuba by United States forces. I thought this was incorrect; I vaguely recalled the landing forces were mostly Cuban exiles, but I passed on the exchange. I was more interested in the beer, anyway. President Kennedy and his administration were vilified. After about a half hour, the whole thing had become seriously boring. While I was no expert, most of the members did not seem to have any idea what they were talking about. Lack of facts did not discourage anyone from expressing a passionate opinion. Even Dale piped up about something after a couple of brews, but I wasn't paying much attention. With the help of the lager we were able to get through the whole affair. I believe the entire meeting took almost an hour and a half; it seemed like three.

Tired and a little high, we left when the group adjourned after promising to come to the next month's meeting. Walking back to campus, it was as though we'd seen a bad movie. It went without saying that our single Bolshevik exposure had been more than enough.

"Wasn't even any vodka, for Chrissake," Jeffrey said.

The night had grown cool. A nighttime haze had drifted in like so much gauze; a few stars shone dimly through the vault. I remember thinking there were no goals set, no agendas defined, no action plan devised. The whole thing was purposeless. I said as much to Dale and Jeffrey.

"Kind of like your life," said Dale. "You should really like it." A real comedian. Well, that was the end of that, I thought. These guys are no threat to anything at all.

But maybe I was wrong.

Chapter 4

We all leave trails as we navigate our lives. In the spring of 1963, I would have thought mine completely unremarkable. I was no one special, a good student with a winning record on the mound but who otherwise had achieved no great end, accomplished no wondrous deed. I was a shooter, a marksman at the local gun club and the subject of an overdramatized page one story. My name had been recorded on someone's yellow pad as having attended a subversive meeting. Finally, I had taken four years of Spanish. I did not know it, but some people were following trails such as this for dark purposes, pursuing shadowy ends of which I had never dreamed.

In May, then, as my last semester as an undergraduate was coming to a close, I met the man I would come to know as Mr. Smith. The meeting was no accident. We were playing a home game, our last, and I was not scheduled to pitch. I sat in the bullpen with the relievers and other starters not playing that day. Even though I would not be pitching out of rotation, we were all required to be in uniform. I had become a sidearm hurler in high school, following a broken shoulder suffered trying to sweep right end. My fastball tailed sharply into a right hand hitter; it was impossible for me to throw a straight pitch. When I really steamed it in, the ball corkscrewed and rose viciously toward the batter's head. My nickname on the team was "The Barber," after Sal "The Barber" Maglie. Maglie pitched for the Dodgers in the 1950s and had the reputation of 'shaving' the hitters with high, close-in fast balls. I had only the suggestion of a curve ball; the coaches were constantly tutoring me with little improvement. I was more interested in the knuckler. Hoyt Wilhelm had been having success with the knuckleball in both leagues since 1952, and I knew I needed another quality pitch to get to the next level. Most of the staff had fooled around with the knuckler without results; there was a real knack to throwing it well. Mine danced well enough, but I just couldn't throw strikes with any consistency. I had always been very effective over the short haul, but this year I had surprised everybody, including me, by having a couple of complete games under my belt.

The pitching staff was far more entertaining than the fielders and other dugout players. Their lives were governed by superstition and ritual. One carried a rabbit's foot, another wouldn't wash his uniform until he won a game. None would tread on a line. For that matter, I stepped over the chalk myself.

The day it all began, we had a larger than usual contingent of fans, and were idly discussing this from our seats in the right field bullpen. The seats themselves were just folding chairs and not very comfortable. We used to play a game with the chairs. Leaning back so the front legs were off the ground, the object was to see how long one could keep the chair balanced on only the rear two legs. Looking out into the bullpen from behind home plate, the fans could often see a bunch of players tilted back in their chairs, wind milling their arms and legs like mad to keep their chairs in balance. It must have made a funny sight, especially when someone tipped over. Pretty intelligent way to pass the afternoons. With all the time to kill in the bullpen, you'd think we'd read or study, maybe have political discussions or intellectual discourse about great works of literature. We never did, though. There was plenty of moronic conversation, usually about sex or baseball or the latest Mad magazine.

Dewey Langeman, another senior, was our tobacco chewing champion. He could spit it just like the major leaguers on television, in a long brown stream. He was more accurate with his tobacco than his curve ball. A lot of the time, the juice dribbled down his chin onto his uniform. It never seemed to quite come out in the wash. How he stayed on the team was a tribute to university's baseball scouts: they couldn't recruit anyone better. Some of the rest of us had tried a chew. It made me sick and irritated my mouth too much.

"Must be three hundred and fifty people here," Dewey said. There was more like a hundred and fifty. Still, a big crowd for us. "They must think I'm going in."

That was pretty funny. Only Dewey's mom would be in the stands if he was going to pitch that day.

The afternoon grew warm, and the sounds of baseball made me sleepy. I think that's always been part of the appeal of our national pastime to me. I must have dozed on the folding chair for an inning or so. It wouldn't have been the first time. From the bullpen, the sun had drifted towards first base when the game ended. Trailing our lengthening shadows, we headed toward the showers. I hadn't thrown a pitch, and neither had most of the staff, but we all showered anyway. It was part of baseball. About a half hour later, we came out in groups of two or three, eventually splitting up as we headed towards our separate fraternities or living groups. I was walking with Dick Appleby and Don Newsome; they split off at the path in front of the University Center toward their fraternity. It was now about 4:30. Alone, I headed towards my fraternity when I heard my name called.

To this day, I wish I hadn't.

"Mr. D___!" I turned and saw a slender, well-dressed man about five paces behind me. He looked to be about my height. His coat and tie told me he was a scout. Or at least that's what I thought. Somehow, he looked familiar.

"Yes?" I stopped to let him catch up. The scout had a friendly smile and he stuck out his hand. "My name is Smith. I enjoyed the game."

My heart started to pound. This guy was from the Yankees, or maybe the Pirates. The Yankee pitching was not quite what it used to be. My mind raced. Maybe I would meet my pitching hero, Whitey Ford. Could I pick my uniform number? Their bullpen staff had a lot of numbers in the 50's. Bonus baby? Frank Leja and Tom Carroll. Two guys never heard from again but who signed for big bucks with the Yanks. He must be from New York with a coat and tie. Am I on my way?

"You did? Did you see my last start?" I had pitched a four-hit complete game, with two walks. Two of the hits were just infield singles.

"No, actually, I didn't," he replied. Oh, damn. Had he heard about it?

"Who do you represent?" I asked. This seemed to take him aback for a second.

"What do you mean?"

"What team? Aren't you a scout? A baseball scout?"

The Man on the Grassy Knoll

Comprehension dawned on Mr. Smith. "Oh, no, not really," he said. My heart sank back down my throat. What did this guy want?

"No, I don't work for a baseball team," he continued. "But I'd like to talk with you about something else. Can I buy you a cup of coffee?"

I didn't drink coffee. "You can buy me a soda," I told him. I could have used a beer but of course the University Center cafeteria didn't sell beer.

"Fine," he said. Instead of heading into the U.C., though, he turned toward the parking lot. "I know a place just off campus."

He named an expensive restaurant, Café Sauvignon. I had heard of the place but had never been there. Neither had most students. One *dined* at the Café Sauvignon. I just ate in the fraternity dining room, a kind of mess hall. Our refrigerator had a big padlock and chain on it. Once in a great while somebody would get a pair of bolt cutters if he was really hungry.

I was impressed but at the same time cautious. Who was this guy? Not some queer, I prayed fervently. Ray Dawkins, our first baseman, had run into a fag in some downtown bar three or four months earlier. It had been an unpleasant experience all around, involving an ambulance and a couple of cops.

Mr. Smith walked to a white Impala in the parking lot. He stood very erect, and had a no-nonsense air about him. He motioned for me to get in.

"Please," he said. I got in the passenger side. The car smelled new. The Impala was a nice automobile, and we were going to a classy restaurant. If Mr. Smith was trying to impress me, he was succeeding. I was going to let him do the talking, but he didn't say much until we reached our destination, just a few minutes away. As we entered, I felt underdressed in my button down shirt and khaki pants, with the little belt in the back - the uniform of the early 1960's. I was starting to get hungry just by association, although it wasn't even dark yet.

The maitre d' was apparently not yet on duty. There was no one seated in the lavishly appointed dining room. Mr. Smith motioned me into the bar, where we sat in the end booth. Evidently he wanted some privacy. It didn't really matter, anyway, since there were only two other people in the place and they were at the bar.

The waiter arrived. As Mr. Smith ordered a martini, I studied my new acquaintance. He was perhaps 6"2" or 6'3", and looked a trim 190 pounds or so. It dawned on me why he'd seemed familiar; he looked like Randolph Scott, the movie actor. I got the impression he might have been an athlete in his youth. Mr. Smith was an expensive dresser, although my collegiate wardrobe would not qualify me as an expert. His tie looked like it cost more than my only suit, a Cricketeer with two pairs of pants. His tailored white shirt did not have a front pocket. I pegged him as in his late 30's, perhaps early 40's. His hair was brown, close-cropped, and just beginning to show flecks of gray. He had an engaging smile. The word that came to mind was smooth.

I got adventurous and ordered a Bloody Mary. Heck, I wasn't paying. In a few minutes, the waiter brought our drinks. Mr. Smith sipped his martini and nodded in appreciation. I was in no hurry if he wasn't; the atmosphere was really nice and I was enjoying the drink. This bartender made a much better Bloody Mary than the fraternity sophomores assigned bartending duty back on campus.

Mr. Smith took another sip, set down his martini, and leaned forward. "Mr. D___, as I said, I don't work for a baseball team. If someone is scouting you for professional baseball, that's great but it isn't me. I'm here for another reason."

He took another sip while I inspected the groceries in my drink. All I needed was peanut butter for the celery stalk.

"Mr. D___, I work for the federal government. A special branch of the federal government. We do very specialized work and sometimes it takes a long time to find the best person for a particularly difficult job. Sometimes we need a special skill that does not exist on the inside. Even if we can locate a particular talent within, we might find we cannot use the person because of their connection to other employees or branches, if you know what I mean."

I had no idea what he meant. He swirled his martini and continued.

"The job might be too sensitive. The need for secrecy is sometimes of the highest possible magnitude."

What the hell was this? I thought incredulously. The federal government needs a pitcher? He talked like somebody out of a B movie. Maybe he *was* Randolph Scott.

Smith/Scott continued. "Let me ask you a question before we go any further, all right? Your draft board has classified you as 1-Y. What's that all about? What's the matter with your shoulder?"

I was astonished. "You know about that? What the hell... Who are you?" Getting my draft status was amazing enough, but he knew the reason, which meant he probably had seen the records, I deduced.

"As I said, I'll explain in a moment. Please answer the question."

"Well, it's the damnedest thing," I said. "I broke my shoulder playing football in high school, and now - "

I stopped as a thought occurred to me. Maybe this guy was an Army investigator or something. He must have read it in my face.

"Please. I'm not here to question your status."

"Well, I can pop it in and out at will. It doesn't hurt."

Mr. Smith smiled. "And naturally you popped it out when they gave you your draft physical, and told them it happened all the time, and it hurt like hell."

I didn't answer directly. I wondered if I had made a mistake going with this person.

"My whole military experience was just that one day, and I didn't like it much. They had box lunches, but you didn't get one if you failed the physical." I recalled that. Cheap bastards. "What's that got to do with anything? You sure you're not a scout?"

"So it doesn't interfere with anything, then? It never pops out when you're pitching? Or shooting?"

Again, I was taken aback. Who *was* this guy?

"No, it doesn't affect that either, except that I think that's why I throw mostly sidearm. Scares the crap out of right-handed batters. It doesn't affect anything, except two years out of my life if they would've drafted me. How do you know about my shooting?"

Smith continued. "Well, they wouldn't draft you while you're in college, would they?"

27

The Man on the Grassy Knoll

Or law school, I had been pretty sure, but now of course it didn't matter. With my 1-Y status, I was golden.

"You have some very special talents, Mr. D___." He paused and sipped his drink. "Unique and special talents," he repeated.

"This is a joke, right?" I said. Suddenly I got it. Spears or Elliot or some guys on the ball team had gotten this guy to con me. "Was it Spears? Elliot? Both of them? They guys from the team? Must be the team. You met me at the ballpark." I babbled on.

Smith looked serious. I mean, he looked deadly serious. "This is no joke, Mr. D___. No joke at all. If you find this is funny, then perhaps we made a mistake."

I backpedalled. "Well, no," I heard myself saying. "Hang on a minute. It's just hard to believe what you're saying. This stuff doesn't happen every day, you know. At least, not to me."

He seemed to relax a little. "I suppose not."

I took my cue.

"What talents do I have? Just what branch of the government did you say you worked for, Mr. Smith?" I picked up my empty drink glass and swirled the ice. Smith signaled for the waiter. After ordering another round for both of us, he continued.

"You're pretty good with a weapon, aren't you?" he asked, reaching into his jacket pocket. Suddenly I felt a chill in that lounge. It wasn't the ice.

"What do you mean?" I asked, inanely. What else could he mean?

He unfolded the page one article from back in March, the one that said I was a crack shot with lightning reflexes and

NRA national champ. "Good with a rifle." He nodded as he looked at the photo. "Very quick. Accurate. Amazing story."

Amazing, all right. Part of it wasn't even true.

"So are a million other guys. Lots of them probably work for you." My mind was racing a zillion miles an hour, but it was out of gear. I had no clue where he was going. The second round of drinks arrived and I downed half of mine in one gulp. *Had I ignored something in the mail? Was my draft card in my wallet?* It said to carry it on my person at all times, even though I was 1-Y.

"You want me to enter some sort of international rifle competition?" I asked, not really believing that. The Olympics were a year or so off, and I had no illusions I was a world-class marksman. I probably wouldn't even place in the nationals.

"No, it's not that sort of thing we have in mind. We have other reasons why this job is so specialized, and why you uniquely qualify. I'll explain this all to you," he said. Evidently he didn't mean right now. "We would like you to think about doing some work for us."

He reminded me that my second question had not been answered. "What branch of the federal government do you work for?" I asked again.

Mr. Smith said, "In order for me to go much further we're going to have to execute a document which binds you to secrecy. You are not to repeat anything you hear from me."

A couple entered the bar and sat at another booth. Maybe twenty feet away, somebody was still living a normal life.

"Can I see some identification?" I asked, probably belatedly. Mr. Smith reached into his jacket pocket and extracted a black leather fold over wallet. He flipped it open and I saw a badge and what appeared to be a federal identification card. Of course, I had no idea what a federal identification card was supposed to look like, but this looked like one. I believe the badge said Department of the Treasury, or U.S. Treasury, or something similar, but it was just an impression. As for the card, I couldn't read any of it. I leaned forward but Smith folded it away.

"The Cold War is the most serious threat to the civilized world mankind has ever seen," said Mr. Smith.

I indicated my agreement. This whole thing was so surreal I felt as though I were hearing myself speak, while my mind was still trying to comprehend the situation.

"The American people must be protected. Sometimes the means required to protect them fall outside the Constitutional boundaries. Do you believe that?" he asked.

"You mean like tapping phones and opening mail and things like that?" I asked. I knew damned well he meant more than that; why else was he talking to a sharpshooter?

"Things like that," he replied. As I said, I could think of a few additional 'means'.

"Sure," I said. A new thought was bothering me. I continued. "I can't believe you would just contact a guy like this without knowing a hell of a lot more about me than my shooting skills," I said. "How do you know where I might go with this conversation? How would you know you could trust me?"

Actually, I had no idea where I could go with this conversation. Maybe nowhere. He probably already knew that.

"Mr. D___, we do know something about your background. We know quite a bit about you. Yes. We know about your marksmanship, don't we? You are a solid citizen and a loyal American. Young people like you are the future hope of our nation." That was nice. I liked to think it was true. So I was a loyal American and I could shoot straight.

There was a silence for a few minutes. Mr. Smith was content to watch me; I am sure a panoply of emotions played across my face. I had a zillion questions but I was not sure what most of them were.

Finally I spoke. "I need to know a lot more about you and your organization before I can make up my mind about this. Of course, I need to know a lot more about what I am supposed to shoot at." There was no sense playing dumber than I actually was.

Mr. Smith replied, "Of course, that is very sensible and completely understandable. Please keep in mind I never said anything about shooting at anything. Don't jump to conclusions. All I need to know for right now is that we have a basis to continue. I know I don't have to tell you this meeting must not be mentioned to anyone."

Curiosity killed the cat. I had to admit to a sense of adventure and perhaps a thrill of the unknown. My life wasn't *that* exciting.

Smith looked at his gold, understated watch. The band was made from some reptile. Whatever he did, it apparently paid well. "Look, I know you have to get back for supper. Why don't you think this over and we can get together again tomorrow evening?"

That was all right with me. I did want to think over our strange conversation, anyway, brief as it had been. We agreed to meet the next day at 7:30 p.m. in the parking lot of the University Center. The parking lot seemed a little cloak-and-dagger.

Back in my room, in the cold light of my study lamp, I tried to figure out who Smith might really be and what he wanted. Clearly, I was supposed to shoot somebody. Why me? The story really didn't wash. The military had thousands of sharpshooters, as I had told Smith, and there were outfits in the service branches filled with clandestine operative type guys. At least, I thought there had to be. Was he CIA? Did they get Treasury badges? Maybe I read it wrong, or maybe that was cover. When would you ever have to flash a CIA badge? Giving somebody a speeding ticket on the autobahn? No, they didn't have speed limits on the autobahn, as I remembered.

Most likely he was fake. It just didn't make sense to go outside the government unless he wasn't part of the government. But was that wrong? Didn't sometimes the secret branches recruit from the outside, when they needed something requiring special skills or the situation was very sensitive? Or maybe because the guy doing the job was expendable. Oh, Christ. Maybe that was it. If you used a soldier, or some black operations squad, you couldn't very well eliminate them after the job. Either Smith was phony or the job was so dangerous or sensitive the mission guy was not going to be around afterward.

This had nothing to do with the question I had not even considered yet. Could I really shoot somebody? Some living breathing person, no matter how much of an enemy he was? I supposed I could do it during a war, when my own life would be on the line, but this was going to be different. I really didn't think I could just ice somebody in cold blood. Or could I?

I made a mental note to check Mr. Smith's license plates.   If his story checked out, he would be sporting government plates. Or would he, actually? If he worked for a clandestine organization he wouldn't have government plates at all. But he would have blackwall tires, I'd bet. My thoughts grew fuzzy. It was late.

What the hell did I know?   This wasn't doing me much good. Finals were right around the corner and I had enough distractions. I fell into a troubled sleep around 1 or 1:30 a.m.

Chapter 5

The next day passed uneventfully. Doing routine things, in my comparatively sane and orderly environment, I almost began to believe Mr. Smith had not intruded into my life at all. Certainly I was skeptical about his purposes. I decided I needed to be firmer in my demeanor, put him on the defensive. He had put me off-balance. Who wouldn't be, with such a crazy story? Maybe I shouldn't even go, I thought. Although if he was just a nut job, he wouldn't have known about my draft status, would he? He didn't really sound crazy. I wanted some more documentation.

After dinner, I wandered down to the University Center parking lot. Again, it was another wonderful spring evening. The fragrances of blooming flowers and growing grass seemed the sweet essence of life itself. I wondered if Mr. Smith would show at all. I didn't have to wonder very long because promptly at 7:30 his Chevrolet pulled up. He leaned over and opened the passenger door, and I got in.

As we drove off campus, Mr. Smith was cordial. "I suppose I gave you enough to think about yesterday, didn't I?"

"Yeah," I replied. "Sure you did. The subject's been on my mind all day."

"I'll try to answer most of your questions tonight," he said.

"I can't take too long. Are we going far? I've got to study," I told him. "Finals start next week."

"Please," he said. "I'll make this as quick as I can and then I won't bother you until after graduation. Unless, of course, you don't wish to pursue this any further."

Smith headed across town, turning left by the newspaper building and then took the highway to a motel near the city limits. He had the windows open in the gorgeous weather. There was little traffic; the trip took less than fifteen minutes. We exchanged small talk, mostly; it seemed we weren't going to discuss sensitive matters before we got wherever we were going. He pulled into the parking lot. When we got out of his car, Smith unlocked the trunk and extracted a manila envelope. He tucked it under his arm and we entered the building. I figured he was staying at this motel. We went into the bar and sat at a round booth. The place was dark and pretty deserted; there were maybe two other patrons watching the television over the bar.

When we had ordered our drinks - I think I asked for a White Russian, with perhaps some irony - Mr. Smith withdrew a sheaf of pages from the manila envelope.

"Mr. D___, you will recall I spoke of signing a document. Actually, there are two documents. I have them here."

"I thought this over," I said, "and I don't think I can sign until you've answered a few more questions." This seemed a prudent approach.

"I understand your reasoning," said Smith, "but unfortunately we need the secrecy agreement signed before we can go any further."

So. Mr. Smith was not going to be pushed. Did this make him more credible or less so? Maybe more, actually.

"I don't know."

"I am sorry, but that's the way it is. I don't make the rules."

What the hell. Maybe that was true.

"Well, let me see the agreements," I said.

Smith passed them over. The first was a form entitled Authorization to Release Information. This was followed by a questionnaire, several pages in length. There were spaces for references; Smith or someone had crossed them out. There was a business card attached to the first page. It read:

Edward Smith

Smith Enterprises

Below was an address and telephone number. I believe the address was on N Street in Washington.

"This is you?" I asked, pointing to the card.

"Actually, that's an old card," he said. "Don't keep it. I'll get you a current one."

"Is this your office?" I asked.

"Like I said, I'll get you a current card."

Anyone could get business cards, though, couldn't they?

I looked through the Authorization form and questionnaire again. "I thought you knew everything about me already," I said, flipping the pages.

He shrugged. "This one's just necessary paperwork," he said, "for the files."

Files? That didn't sound so clandestine after all. But when I looked at the second document, I reconsidered. The two page paper covered their asses, but not mine. It bound me to total secrecy and went on to hold the United States of America harmless, should I incur any injury from my activity. The risks were mine. I interpreted the language to include incarceration, death and/or dismemberment. This thing was really spooking me.

"Mr. Smith, I'm at a disadvantage. I'm not a lawyer and normally I guess I'd take this agreement to one. I don't think you want me to do that, though. Frankly, this thing is so one-sided I'm not sure if I want to sign this or not." I was pretty sure I didn't.

Mr. Smith smiled. "There is one thing we have not discussed yet. That is your compensation."

Compensation? I hadn't gotten that far in my thinking. I guess I thought they wanted me to work for the patriotic value.

"What?" I asked. That's all I could think of to ask, except maybe how much. "How much are we talking about?"

"I can discuss all this after you sign the secrecy agreement. The other you can take with you and fill out over the next day or so."

Still, I hesitated.

"Remember, you aren't signing anything requiring you to do anything. It just requires you to maintain secrecy."

That was true. I wasn't committing to do anything. All I was committing to do was not talk about it. If I found out Smith was a phony, the document wouldn't mean anything anyway, and I could tell the authorities. Not that anyone would listen to Smith's crazy story, anyway. Especially since it would be my crazy story, I realized.

So I signed. Wouldn't you?

  *   *   *   *   *

The Man on the Grassy Knoll

Mr. Smith took back the signed secrecy agreement and put it back in the manila envelope. He smiled.

"Mr. D___, the United States is prepared to pay you a total of $60,000 for helping us. There would be a $15,000 down payment, and another $45,000 upon completion of the assignment."

My God. I was dumbfounded. I am sure my jaw was slack. Smith regarded me with amusement as my wheels churned. $60,000 was a fortune. I had been hoping to make maybe $9,000 or $10,000 for the year after graduation. Smith was offering me six or seven years pay for "an assignment." I was certain now I was going to have to shoot somebody. The Pope? I wouldn't shoot the Pope for any amount of money. The Teamsters Union guy? Khrushchev?

I was close.

I asked the first question that popped into my mind. "How long is this assignment going to last?"

"Not very long," was his reply. "Everything should be completed before the end of the year."

He had me in tow. Still, I pushed Mr. Smith. "I want half down. $30,000."

"Okay. Agreed," he said. That caught me up short.

"The money will have to go into an offshore account," said Mr. Smith. "You'll understand why after things are explained. Also, there'll be time and amount limits on withdrawals afterward." We seemed to have concluded our haggling, and I didn't even know what I was supposed to do. I wasn't ready.

I had a student checking account with about $40 in it. I had no knowledge of "offshore accounts" and the like. Sometimes I'm a fast learner, though.

"One thing. Where's my copy of the agreement?"
Mr. Smith smiled again. 'You don't get a copy."

Chapter 6

I mentioned Mr. Smith to no one. The next day, between classes, I filled out the personal history form for Smith's "files". I had to list all my residences for the past fifteen years, which was pretty easy. So was the part about past employment. I figured they didn't want the summer jobs. Then there was a section asking if I had ever been connected to a variety of unsavory organizations, indicted, bankrupt, currently under charges - I was tempted to write NOT YET - , and so on. I began to feel pretty good about myself with all the NO's I was writing. All in all, I was done in about fifteen minutes. I shoved the completed form in a textbook and awaited Mr. Smith's next communication. I was now preoccupied with studying for my exams, so when I didn't hear from Smith for two or three days, I didn't give it much thought.

When he did call me, it was to set up a meeting two days hence. It struck me that I hadn't given Mr. Smith the name of my fraternity or phone number. We worked out the time, which wasn't easy as things really were hectic now. Finals were in full swing. Again he picked me up in the U.C. parking lot. I believe it was a Tuesday evening. After 5 p.m., the lot got little traffic and apparently Mr. Smith wasn't too worried about us being noticed together there.

The Man on the Grassy Knoll

This time we went to the Westridge Hotel, in the downtown area. Like the other places we had been, this was not a student hangout. We were seated in a back booth of the lobby bar. I was getting used to this. I ordered a beer, and Mr. Smith did the same. After they arrived, I pulled out the completed disclosure form and handed it to Mr. Smith. He looked it over briefly.

"Good," he said, tucking it away. "All right. I believe everything is in order. Let me tell you how we would like to proceed.

'As I had told you earlier, these are difficult and dangerous times. The United States is the bastion of the free world. It's hackneyed, I know, but still true. Our allies don't always make things easier. They bicker with us but hide under our skirts as soon as the hammer rattles against the sickle. We have a heavy responsibility. There are many individuals and organizations, even nations, who would take advantage of our liberties and use this advantage to pursue their ends against us. Some of these enemies are easily identifiable, and some are not. Some are within.

'In order to maintain our security and keep our vigilance, it is sometimes necessary to proceed outside the letter of the law. I mentioned this the other day. You seemed to understand."

"Well, anyone can see that," I replied. "The question is when does vigilance become abuse?" I hoped that sounded like an intelligent question.

"Exactly. Now for instance you know we have a Communist maniac operating less than a hundred miles from our shores. *Less than a hundred miles.* New York to Philadelphia. Los Angeles to San Diego. We have almost

41

gone to nuclear war over this dangerous situation. However, it is clear from recent history that the normal avenues open to us are not enough. You are up on current events?" he asked.

So Cuba was the subject. "Reasonably, I guess. I mean, who doesn't know about Cuba?" They must have known I speak Spanish. *Que lindo.*

"What the press reports and what really happens aren't always the same. Sometimes they're not even close." I could believe that. "Sometimes things are classified for everyone's protection. A situation might be gravely dangerous and the public wouldn't know. In this particular situation, we are going to have to pull out all the stops."

"Pull out all the stops?" I echoed.

"You're a smart young man, Mr. D___. Your SAT's tell us so. Did you not think you were correct as to why we approached you?"

So now there was no doubt. It was one thing to speculate, another to hear it confirmed. I was getting rubbery legged, and I was sitting down.

"So I am supposed to take somebody out," I said. It no longer was a question.

Mr. Smith did not reply. Music was coming from somewhere. I hadn't noticed when it had started. I recall it was Unchained Melody by Al Hibbler. Somehow it seemed out of kilter, now. Everything seemed a little out of kilter now.

It had to be Castro, or that other guy in the news. How the hell was I supposed to do that? "I don't suppose it takes a genius to figure out who this somebody is," I said.

Mr. Smith leaned forward and lowered his voice, which hadn't been loud anyway. His immaculate shirts didn't seem to wrinkle, I saw. They almost glowed, they were so white.

"We have already tried to take this somebody out. More than once. We have not succeeded. And, by the way, that is never to be repeated."

"How?" I asked.

"Not with a gun. We have had to be concerned about repercussions."

"But not now?" Smith just looked at me.

"With what then?" I asked. Rockets?

"I won't get into that. Do you see now that if this person is removed with a weapon, an overt action that is clearly not natural or accidental, we cannot possibly afford any connection with the United States government? No matter if it succeeds or fails? Absolutely no traceable contact at all, whether military or not? Can you see what is likely to happen then?"

I guess I could indeed.

"The Cuban intelligence organization is no banana republic joke, Mr. D___. And they have plenty of help from Moscow. Our own intelligence community is not totally leak proof, either."

Boy, things were happening fast. I needed to slow down. Perhaps Smith sensed that.

"I know you are in the midst of your exams. Nothing is going to happen for awhile. You know what kind of mission this is. I won't kid you; there might be some danger. Like I told you, I won't bother you again until after finals. Mull it over until then. I will contact you right before graduation for your decision. If you decide to help us, we will get to work right away and the money will be deposited in your name. If not, that's the end of it and we'll part company."

So that's how we left it. We finished our beers and exchanged a few minutes of small talk. I was finding Mr. Smith skilled in the conversational arts, without ever saying anything about himself. Afterward, he dropped me back in the U.C. parking lot and I did not see him again for two weeks. I was now convinced my new friend was the genuine article.

As graduation approached, I still had no job. I had no steady girlfriend at the moment, no entanglements complicating my life. I had a few bucks and an old car which wasn't running too well. Worst of all, my baseball career was over - I could look forward to playing softball in some old men's league wearing a uniform advertising a dry cleaners or insurance agency. The best and brightest of us were going to work for $12,000, tops. I had that beat by a mile. I remembered Ramon telling me how his family got screwed by Castro; how they'd lost most of what they had to the revolution. Maybe it was payback time. Wouldn't it be something if I succeeded and could find Mirasol and tell her? And Ramon and his parents?

Christ, I thought. I'm graduating college and I still think like a high school kid. I'd never be able to tell anyone. Still, that would be amazing.

Once I got used to the idea of danger, the future seemed more exciting than daunting. If only I could tell my Mom.

Wouldn't she be proud?

Chapter 7

Graduation: a gorgeous, sunny June day. Green leaves and pastel flowers everywhere. My university really has a beautiful campus. It was hot, and so many of us wore shorts under our gowns. My folks and a few other family members were in attendance. The speeches were long and without redeeming value to me or my nearby classmates, many of whose heads lolled and jerked as the afternoon droned on like so many flies. The procession of students trudging to the podium to receive the dummy diploma and perfunctory handshake dragged on for, it seemed, geologic time. Mercifully, the ceremonies ended before nightfall. I found my Mom thought everything thrilling.

"Oh, did you hear Dr. M_____'s speech?" she gushed.

"Sure, mom. Did you like it?" I sort of heard it, but I hadn't been listening.

My mom spoke in italics a lot. "It was so *relevant*," she said. Probably not to me, I thought, considering my new career. "What an exciting time in your life." She didn't know the half of it.

My family was staying downtown at the Regency, just a block or two from the restaurant where Mr. Smith and I had our first heart-to-heart. They had come up for Graduation Weekend. The school had sent out a list of recommended lodgings for parents and friends, and the Regency was probably the classiest. We celebrated my graduation with dinner in their main dining room. There were cherubs or baby angels on the ceiling. Done in gold, they looked like they belonged there. An attractive woman in a long red low-cut dress was playing lilting music on the harp. There were thirteen of us. It was all quite nice until I had a random thought as we ate: Was this my personal Last Supper? The analogy started to spook me, especially as I gazed up at the ceiling; the angels almost seemed to float.

My father asked about prospective job offers. I told him I thought I was going to accept a job with the government. I gave him a brief outline of the position, which was my cover story as supplied by Mr. Smith, but no details.

"Amateurs fill in too many details when they lie," Smith had said. "Nobody wants the details anyway and they'll just trip you up. A good lie is mostly truth."

"I imagine traveling will be exciting at first," said my father. He had traveled through France, riding on a tank turret. I imagine that was pretty exciting, at first.

"Well, I haven't really seen that much of the country, and I have the chance to do it now, while I'm single."

Mom was getting worried about the road. Would I eat right? Would I get robbed in some hotel? What kind of social life would I have on the road? Actually, I wondered the same things.

"It's only for the rest of the year, Mom. Until I'm familiar with things in the field. Don't worry, I'll try and call you every week."

"You'll *try?* Every *week?*"

46

The Man on the Grassy Knoll

Yeah, Mom. From Havana. The Hilton. Or maybe prison. I would guess making a person-to-person call from some Cuban dungeon would be a hell of a trick.

"Not too many details," Smith had reiterated. "People, even family, aren't *that* curious."

I was supposed to be working for an unspecified branch of the federal government that would take me through the National Park system. Under this scenario, I would be unavailable by phone for days at a time, without causing undue alarm. Mr. Smith said he could provide a Washington phone number for messages, if I wanted. This job seemed a little far afield from my major course of study (Faulkner? Beowulf?), but I explained it away well enough. Smith was right. It's all how you tell it.

I had serious misgivings during that weekend. I felt a new distance between me and my family, and it bothered me. Yet, at the same time, I felt very close. It's hard to explain. If I were successful, they would never know anything about it. If not, I could only speculate as to what, if anything, I would tell them. Or what somebody else would tell them if I wasn't around to do it. In those precious few days, I enjoyed my family more than they could know.

On Sunday, after church, I said goodbye to my alma mater with one last ride around the campus. Church was usually limited to important Sundays and parental visits, but I enjoyed that day's final service. I also said goodbye to a lot of fond memories, good friends, lazy, warm afternoons of varsity baseball, with the sweet smells of spring and new-mown grass wafting across the diamond, and a life of little real responsibility. I was going to miss it all very much.

The Man on the Grassy Knoll

I had so much stuff we had to ship some of it; the rest went in the station wagon and my '56 Olds 98 with the special no-wax paint job that had faded badly. Then we all drove home. I had a week before leaving for my new job. Mr. Smith had given me a thousand dollar advance for expenses, and we were going to go 'offshore' to consummate our transaction. Mr. Smith said he would handle all the details, which I supposed meant getting me a passport.

Back home, I felt the same bittersweet emotions as I spent that last free time with my old high school friends. Some were already working out of town, and others were on vacation, but I did see several of my buddies for what might be the last time. I took Mary Anne Winter to the movies. I had been taking Mary Anne Winter to the movies for about eight years, off and on. She always figured out what was going to happen and explained things to me when I couldn't follow the plot. It got so that I could hardly go the movies at all without her. It all seemed so normal and regular and a zillion miles away from where they wore camouflage and didn't have much of a sense of humor and incarcerated people because they expressed another point of view. Or worse.

Everybody I talked to had normal things in their future. I had a rendezvous with a bearded guy in fatigues.

Or so I thought.

Chapter 8

I packed for an extended trip. I took my only suit, the Cricketeer with two pairs of pants. I'd worn it maybe four times, but didn't know if I'd need it. Anyway, I thought it might look odd if I left it in the closet. After all, I was supposed to be starting, as Mom said, my *career*. My father volunteered to take me to the airport. I could tell this was bothering him, just like when I had left home for college. Another rite of passage. They're awful, really. I needed to get out of there. It was raining, a daylong drizzle that really made me feel depressed. We pulled to the curb by my airline. There was an overhang, but not wide enough to prevent me from getting wet. I leaned sideways to open the door. My dad held up his hand for me to wait a minute.

"Call like you promised, son," he said. "You know your mother will be worried if you don't."

"Sure. Just remember when I'm in the field I can't always get to a phone. I'll be okay." I hoped.

We said hurried good-byes. Men are really lousy at that sort of thing. He pressed an envelope into my hand.

"What's this?" I looked at the envelope, dreading the likelihood that it contained money.

"Just in case you need something unexpected," he said. Oh, shit. This was my low point. I had more money in my bag than I needed, and here he was giving me an envelope. Goddamn it.

"Dad, I really am okay. They're paying me pretty well. I don't need anything," I said, helplessly.

"I know what the government pays," he said. But he didn't, did he?

I swear I almost cried. "Thanks, Dad." That's all I could say. I waved goodbye, smiled, and jumped out into the rain. I grabbed my bags from the back seat and ran into the terminal, toward God-knows-what and Mr. Smith.

$$* \quad * \quad * \quad * \quad * \quad *$$

Nassau was quite a change. The sun was brilliant, the low, cotton cumulus clouds were white as snow, and my shirt was sticking to my back. I was standing in a steam room, bathed in dazzling sunlight. I squinted, even with my good sunglasses on. Mr. Smith and I entered through Immigration and exited the terminal, where a host of taxi drivers competed for our business. I had been very nervous about using the phony identification he had provided, but everything went okay. My first big test at being a government operative. We got into a battered, dusty vehicle of ancient vintage.

Mr. Smith had not given an elaborate explanation, but he did say there were a number of choices as to where we could shelter my funds. The Bahamas was one, and it was easy to get to. Traceability, or the lack of it, was of course the key.

All along the route from the airport, riding on the wrong side of the road (although, oddly, the steering wheel was on the American side), I gazed with interest at the Bahamian scenery. The route, paralleling the coast for a good distance, afforded views of the choppy, blue-green waters and colorful Bahamian houses. I took it all in. It was very beautiful.

"Do you get here often?" I inquired of Mr. Smith. He had doffed his normal business suit jacket in favor of a sport shirt. He didn't quite look the same.

"Not really," he said. "It's another world, isn't it?" It was like nothing I'd ever seen.

We were approaching the downtown area on Bay Street. All of a sudden we were in a miniature traffic jam. There seemed to be only about a dozen small streets in this compact area, but that's where all the vehicles were. Most were tiny European or English cars with those funny translucent headlights. I saw my first Bahamian police officer, or maybe he was English. Resplendent in his tall white helmet, immaculate jacket, dark blue pants with red stripe, he was impressive. Leave it to the British. I watched the Union Jack, on a flagpole up the hill from Bay Street, flutter in the light ocean breeze.

We were to stay one night in New Providence. The banks were already closed, so we had nothing much to do until the next day. That was fine with me. Our hotel was small, with perhaps ten or twelve rooms, and was not air conditioned. I believe it was on Parliament Street, or possibly it was the Parliament Hotel. Wicker and lace. So different from what I was used to. I decided I liked it, if it weren't so sticky. The large windows and fans helped, but I perspired constantly. I was not used to this weather at all.

After we freshened up, Mr. Smith and I took a stroll down to Bay Street. I noticed that the people on the sidewalks fell into a right hand traffic pattern, unlike the cars. I supposed left hand traffic was really unnatural, even to the British.

The Man on the Grassy Knoll

There were a lot of large Bahamian women in loose, colorful dresses selling straw hats and straw suitcases, beads and trinkets. They did not wait to see if we wanted any of their wares; they just pressed their goods on us. I wasn't used to that, either. The ladies hawked their merchandise in loud, lilting voices. It took me awhile to realize they were speaking in a kind of English. Perfume and jewelry shops were numerous.

Then I almost got killed.

We decided to walk down to the waterfront. I stepped off the curb to cross the street when I felt Mr. Smith's arm jerk me back on the sidewalk. A lorry, he called it, sped by right where I was standing.

"Look to the right."

"Thanks."

I was a little shook up. I had, without thinking, looked the wrong way when I stepped off the curb. After that, I looked both ways because I kept getting confused.

Mr. Smith and I were becoming fast friends, in a bizarre way, especially after he saved my life. I was hoping he liked me because I really wanted the other half of my money, and also I didn't want to find out he had other plans for me should things go awry.

We reached the docks. I could look right down to the bottom, as clear as day. I supposed it was about six feet. Mr. Smith said it was more like twenty-five. Exotic little tropical fish swam around the pilings. Smith said there were no barnacles in the Bahamas; the water was so fast-moving from the Gulfstream and it was too pure. He was a regular tour guide. Strolling through the dock area, we meandered around alleyways and shops. It all seemed a water-color world; how could anyone not enjoy life here? We found ourselves in front of the jail. The prisoners talked and joked with the people outside. It didn't look too inviting in there. I suppose they weren't enjoying life very much, although laughter floated through the bars.

Back on Bay Street, we stopped in a dark, cool lounge for drinks. The place smelled like old wood with a hundred years' worth of whiskey soaked into it, and maybe a Havana cigar or two. It was not unpleasant.

"You been here before?" I asked, looking around. The walls were a mint green, muted in the darkness. They seemed to glisten, as though they were wet with condensation.

"Relaxing, isn't it?" Mr. Smith replied, with his usual non-answer answer.

The fans overhead droned on as we sat in the dankness. The place was making me drowsy. In the morning, we would tend to our financial business and fly on to Miami.

"Once we're in Miami, I'm going to have to leave you for a week or two," said Mr. Smith. "I have some other things to do. You'll be staying at the Traveler's Hotel near the airport," he said. "You don't need to hang by the phone, but if plans change, I'll call you."

"Am I flying out of Miami?" I asked.

"We'll see," said Smith. "You might be there for awhile." I wondered if Miami would be the jumping off place for Cuba. I asked him that.

"Oh, you may not actually be going to Cuba," he said. I didn't know if Castro traveled much, but I knew he didn't shop in Miami. Smith didn't elaborate.

In a little while, we left the cave-like tavern and wandered back to the hotel to freshen up. In about an hour, we strolled to a restaurant Mr. Smith favored. At his suggestion, we ate a nice meal of snapper and some Bahamian vegetable dish. The supper was quite pleasant. I supposed the Bahamians had a lot of experience preparing fish. Afterward, I tried to read in my room but fell asleep on the crisp, white sheets until dawn. I slept the sleep of the almost rich.

The next morning, after a breakfast featuring real butter and the creamiest milk I had ever tasted, we walked a few blocks to the bank. They seemed to know Mr. Smith there. The banker, a Mr. Pinder, was polite and efficient. He and Mr. Smith handled everything; I just signed where directed. I never actually saw any cash and so I assumed Mr. Smith had a letter of credit or arranged a wire or some kind of transfer. We opened the account in my real name, since, Smith had explained, my phony ID would have a limited life. I was instructed how to withdraw the funds when appropriate, after our work was completed. I also learned how to do things like check the balance by telephone, although later Mr. Smith cautioned me against that. Mr. Pinder verified that money could be wired in and no one had to be there in person to make deposits.

I watched and learned. I was all set now, wasn't I?

We rode under a tropical cloudburst on the way back to the airport. It rained heavily for maybe five minutes until the clouds vanished. Even before we arrived, the sun appeared again, big and hot, leaving a vibrant rainbow against blue sky. We drove through water steaming up from the pavement.

We were back in Miami that afternoon. I was now a well-off guy, even if I hadn't earned it yet. It felt pretty nice. We took a cab to my hotel, which was just a block or two from the airport, and Smith went back for his flight out of Miami. I settled in at Traveler's. It wasn't on the ocean, but it sure beat working. I thought of the tire and rubber company whose clutches I escaped by being such a poor interviewee. Funny how things worked out.

Chapter 9

Smith wanted to talk about weapons.

We were in Houston following our trip to the Bahamas and my Miami vacation. At least, it seemed like a vacation to me. After four years, having nothing to study seemed odd. I felt guilty without a textbook.

I was becoming a real jet-setter.

It was, I believe, the last week in June. Houston seemed an exciting town, but it had the worst roads I'd ever seen. Maybe their concrete was really adobe, or something. Smith had given me instructions on how to travel without leaving a trail. Money was no problem anymore. Boy, was that nice. Smith cautioned me not to overdo things and to forego the first class stuff. That was getting hard already. Before we left for the Bahamas, he had supplied me with identification in the name of John Graves. I wondered if he had chosen the name out of a macabre sense of irony.

"It's best to keep the same first name," he had explained. "You're not trained in this area. If we gave you another first name, you might forget and not answer to it. Also, you might respond to your real name. See what I mean?"

I could indeed. After traveling under the Graves name for awhile, I began to feel relaxed with the alias. Maybe I would be pretty good at this game, I thought.

The Man on the Grassy Knoll

We sat in Smith's hotel room; obviously he wasn't taking his own advice about first class travel. The Auditorium was several notches above standard. He had asked me to come to Texas because he had other business there. Mr. Smith was the neat one. The closet was not quite closed, and everything was hung up and squared away. I wondered if he had been in the military, with his penchant for neatness and erect bearing.

We reviewed the various rifles I had experience with over the years. He ruled them all out.

"Why?" I asked.

"First, you couldn't use anything you already own, could you? Secondly, use of a NATO weapon or an American-made rifle is taking a needless risk. What do you know about Soviet rifles?"

Evidently Mr. Smith was trying to establish a Russian inference, not just the absence of an American presence.

"You mean the AK-47?" I asked.

Everyone knew about the Kalashnikov. This time-tested Russian rifle was indestructible. It used the medium powered 7.62mm cartridge, which minimized recoil. That much I knew. The 47 came from the year it originated.

"Well, yes. Let's leave that for the Russian infantry. What else?"

"I don't know much about Russian stuff. I've never fired any Russian gun. I know they have some Match rifles that are supposed to be pretty accurate," I said. "I think they use them in international competition."

"Aaah," Mr. Smith intoned with approval. "You are the bright one." He could have been teaching school. "You do get good grades, don't you? Well, the Russians manage to make some stuff, as you put it, that works. We think we have something suitable for you."

"What?"

"Ever heard of a Tokarev?"

"I don't think so," I said.

"7.62mm .54 rimmed center fire. SVT1940. Actually you'll have the Match version - the M1940. Available with a variety of Russian scopes from 2.5 to 8 power. Autoloader. The Russians are big on autoloaders. You'll probably like it, because you're used to the T48. They both use the high powered cartridge. The action's similar, but it's older. The FAL uses the same bolt mechanism. Probably the Belgians copied the Tokarev, and beefed it up."

The 1940 would stand for either the year of manufacture or adoption, I knew, so this was not a new weapon. The M prefix meant Match. Sometimes Match rifles were still production line weapons, but specially selected for accuracy. These were usually bolt action, which tended to be slightly more accurate for a number of reasons. They were then grooved, drilled and tapped for scope mounting. Now you had a sniper rifle.

Smith mentioned several other Soviet weapons. He was impressed with the Mosin Nagant bolt action sniper rifle with PE scope, and a modified S.K.S. I thought I had heard of the latter. He said the S.K.S. would be adequate up to around 200 yards. These two guns would be backups if I didn't like the Tokarev.

I had some questions for Mr. Smith. "What are the circumstances? Distance? Night or day? Indoors or out? Moving or stationary? Traversing?"

"Oh, most certainly outdoors. For the other factors, we don't know yet," was his reply.

"Do all three of these take scopes? What about special ammunition?" I asked.

"Forget the special ammo," Smith said. "You'll only need lead core or hollow point." Hollow point would do a great deal of damage, especially on the way out, but there could be some loss in accuracy over distance. The choice might have to be made in the field.

"What about mercury and other stuff?" If anybody would have advanced ammunition, it would be Mr. Smith.

"What for? You've been reading too many spy stories. There's really no advantage. Don't worry. The Tokarev full power cartridge is all you need. Besides, mercury will ruin a gun. Something for you to keep in mind in the future."

Future? This was Mr. Smith's idea of a joke, I supposed. He paused, then looked at me.

"Remember this. If you just hit a shirtsleeve, we want the arm to come off."

I swallowed. Mr. Smith was reminding me of what lay ahead. It wasn't just a paper target, was it?

"What about the scopes?"

"They'll all be equipped with scopes," he replied.

"Since we don't know the circumstances, I think I would prefer four power on all of them. That's probably best for me as an all around instrument." I knew from experience moving targets would present acquisition problems with greater than four power magnification. The same difficulty existed when using fully-powered rounds – the target could be lost due to recoil. The other limiting factor might be the

The Man on the Grassy Knoll

absence of a rifle rest, although that would seem unlikely. The only thing we knew for certain was the ammunition.

"OK. I think the PE is four power, anyhow," Smith said.

There was another subject very dear to me.

"Getaway," I said. "What happens right after the action? Leave the weapon or take it? Do any of these guns come with a folding stock?"

"Only the AK-47 paratrooper version, I believe, and you won't have that. You're probably going to have to tote that rifle the hell out of there."

"Why? Don't you want it left behind?"

"Not necessarily," he replied. "The advantage is the Russian inference. But anything left behind can be dangerous, no matter how careful we are about sanitizing the weapon." Smith brought up something else.

"Fingerprints."

"I've never been printed," I said.

Smith shook his head. "Doesn't matter. It would be an unnecessary link. You either have to wear gloves or bring the gun back with you. One other thing. There's a chance you won't be the only shooter. If we need to, we can probably manage triangulated fire. Even if there's two of you, there may be enough confusion without having to leave the gun as a trail."

I hadn't realized they were considering a team approach. It told me they really didn't have a target site yet.

Something occurred to me. "You must have known what rifle I used before today," I said. "That's why you already picked the Tokarev."

60

Smith just smiled. "Your parents' tax dollars at work."

"What the hell. You already knew about the T48." It made me feel pretty creepy. I wondered if there was much he - or they - didn't know about me. He had just mentioned my parents, and, a couple of minutes ago, my grades. He had known my SAT scores. Maybe Smith even knew about my girlfriends. I wondered what use that could be to anyone. He hadn't been up on my pitching record, though.

There was a pause. Mr. Smith smiled at me.

"I also know you have a lousy curve ball."

Chapter 10

Smith had other tasks for the next few days – I couldn't imagine what they might be - and so I cooled my heels in Houston. Before leaving, he took me to a nondescript place called The Last Concert Café on Nance Street for some "real Tex-Mex", as he described it. He meant the music as well as the food. We had to knock on the door to get in; for some reason they kept the place locked even during mealtime. Smith must have been familiar with the joint because there wasn't even a sign outside. We couldn't really talk because the live music about blasted the building off its foundation. That was all right with me since my thoughts were heavy and troubled. The food was delicious, though. My palate was expanding again.

That evening I sat alone in my hotel room and stared out the window at the Houston landscape. Our discussion about weapons had spooked me, and I'd hoped Mr. Smith hadn't detected anything amiss. After signing on, I'd tried to be professional and businesslike, but it hadn't completely worked. In actuality, I felt more like a kid playing a game where nobody really got hurt. I suppose it was a defense mechanism. It may seem hard to comprehend, but since the beginning I'd avoided really thinking about what the mission was all about. Whenever thoughts of actually shooting someone had crept into my mind, I'd deflected them. Instead,

The Man on the Grassy Knoll

I'd tried to think about patriotism, adventure, danger, the money – anything but actually acquiring a live unarmed human being in my sights and pulling the trigger. I secretly wondered if I could do it. No matter how hard I tried to convince myself I would be on a military mission, we weren't at war, at least overtly. I knew Fidel Castro was a danger to the United States, a rogue dictator who had brought the Soviet Union and its military might into the Western Hemisphere, but really that would be an abstract concept when the time for action came. I wouldn't be in a battle, with people in uniform firing at me and my fellow soldiers. My life wasn't going to be directly at stake, unless things really went awry, and I definitely didn't want to think about that. I wouldn't be part of a unit engaging in a firefight, where everyone was shooting, kill or be killed. I wasn't a grizzled veteran – hell, I hadn't even gone through basic training.

I sat by that hotel window for awhile as the Tex-Mex worked its way through my digestive system and the sky darkened, trying to face my mission head-on, finally. I felt that if I thought about it long enough, if I faced my fears and natural aversion to gunning down a live human being, I could quell the fear and uncertainty and do my job.

Probably.

*   *   *   *   *

I spent part of August in Arizona. The desert is no place to be in summertime, but there I was, nonetheless, practicing with my small arsenal. Evidently it was the rainy season, which flooded the dry creek beds on occasion. Mostly, though, it was around 110 degrees. It didn't seem to bother the Tokarev, except that it got too hot to hold, even though it was in the shade almost all of the time. I was going to use gloves, anyway, to eliminate fingerprints, and I experimented with various kinds, from surgical to lightweight cotton. Handling the ammunition, even with the autoloader, was awkward. If I had to change from standard to hollow point, or vice versa, I was going to have a problem. I was having a hard time, and here I was under no pressure. I could imagine fumbling with the ammunition under actual field conditions. In the end, I discarded the idea of wearing gloves at all. I didn't tell Smith. If I left the rifle, I would try and wipe it down. Besides, what could the Cuban authorities do with my fingerprints? Like I told Smith, I had never been printed. While I was not completely comfortable with that, there really was no good solution.

We had been way outside of town, between Tucson and some place called Ajo, I think. At least that's what Mr. Smith told me. It might have been the moon, judging from the landscape. Mr. Smith was driving a pickup truck, a 1962 Chevy short box. He pulled off the highway and turned past a No Trespassing sign onto a blacktop road. We climbed a gradual hill through the desert for perhaps two or three miles. The asphalt ribbon slipped behind another rise and the road became an unpaved suggestion. We bounced and jangled along for maybe another mile, past stands of tall saguaro. I was awed by the size of these majestic desert cacti; they were much bigger than they seemed from television westerns.

We came to a compound of sorts. There was an Airstream aluminum trailer on the left side, obviously well-traveled, with rounded corners. It looked like an old beer can.

The Man on the Grassy Knoll

Another trailer, similar but slightly smaller, stood off to the right. A dusty pickup was parked next to it. Behind these stood a low half-shed, with a corrugated tin roof. A hill rose beyond the shed, perhaps six hundred yards away. This would be the firing range. A single story ranch house stood about a hundred yards to the left of these structures. It looked clean and tidy.

When we pulled up, a sturdy and unattractive woman appeared outside the smaller trailer. She knew Mr. Smith, who introduced her as Mrs. Dell. Mrs. Dell appeared part Mexican or Indian and the name didn't fit. She could have been anywhere from 45 to 65. Mr. Smith explained that she would be my cook and housekeeper for the time period it took to get proficient with the Tokarev or any other weapon I chose. I would stay in the guest trailer, the larger one on the left. I wondered how they got electricity out where we were, but obviously they did. Power lines ran from the guest trailer in the direction of the ranch house. Whether the ranch house had a generator, or was wired for power, I didn't know. I never saw anyone but Mrs. Dell and never entered the ranch house.

Inside the guest trailer, it was cool and comfortable and surprisingly neat. Perhaps spartan was a more descriptive word. The air conditioning unit seemed a homemade addition. It ran pretty much full time, and was noisy, but did an adequate job. When we went inside, Mr. Smith opened a curtained closet area and took out the three weapons, wrapped in khaki blankets: the Tokarev, the S.K.S., and the Mosin Nagant sniper rifle. I was anxious to inspect all of them. I picked up the Tokarev. The semi-automatic didn't have the heft of my T48.

"Seems a little light," I said. "Like a light Garand."

The Man on the Grassy Knoll

"Think so? It's actually a beefed-up version of the old SVT1938," he replied. "That thing would just about float. Too fragile. Jammed all the time. Plus the magazine sometimes fell out."

The magazine fell out?

"Great. That's comforting."

Smith laughed. "They fixed that problem on this model, though. Listen, the Tokarev wasn't that great under combat conditions. It didn't take much abuse. But it seems well-suited for an application like ours. You'll just have to see which weapon you prefer."

Mounted on all three rifles were 4X scopes, presumably of Russian manufacture. Smith said the Tokarev and S.K.S. had PE scopes. There were also wooden boxes and bricks of 7.62mm ammunition. The Mosin-Nagant and Tokarev used identical 7.62x54mmR cartridges, which was convenient. The S.K.S. fired the lighter 7.62x39mm round. I had enough of both types for a major siege. Everything was plainly marked: military standard or hollow point. Mr. Smith must have figured I was going to need to ventilate the entire hill behind the target area. That's how many rounds I had.

"Have at it," Smith said, gesturing at the pile.

"What, now?" I asked. Smith chuckled again. I guess he found this whole subject amusing.

"No, not now. It's 110 degrees out there. Wait until it gets near dusk. It cools down surprisingly fast. Practice just after dawn. Don't worry about waking anybody. When it gets a little cooler, I'll show you where the lights are for night shooting. They're not bright, and they don't really work well, but if you want to try them, go ahead."

"Were all these scopes original equipment?" I asked.

"I believe so," Smith said, "but I'm not completely sure. Anyway, they're definitely Eastern manufacture."

Boy, I didn't want to be in this hellhole very long. I really had liked Miami and the Bahamas, especially compared to this moonscape.

"Are we far from Mexico?" I asked.

"Not too far from Nogales, but don't get to thinking about it," said Mr. Smith. "Your passport can't be compromised. You'll stay here until you are ready with whichever weapon you want."

In about an hour, Mrs. Dell brought a serviceable supper of tacos and refried beans. Mr. Smith suggested I use the free time beforehand to break down the weapons and get familiar with them while he was still around to help me, since there were no manuals. Actually, I didn't get any farther than the Tokarev. I got the rifle into five or six pieces, but later on I was able to break the weapon into about ten parts. Someone had provided a couple of extra recoil springs, magazines, and a gas regulator adjustment tool. The Tokarev clip held ten rounds in the detachable magazine. Most importantly, the Russian gun had a flash hider. What about a silencer?

"Sorry, no silencer," Smith said. "As far as we know, the Russians never made one for the Tokarev. If we adapt something - and I don't know that we could, anyway - it wouldn't be authentic. We might as well give you the T48, then. Besides, there can be some degradation in performance with a silencer." I didn't know that, but then again I didn't know much about suppressors, anyway. "The flash hider will have to do."

It would do for him, since he wasn't going to be there when it mattered.

The Man on the Grassy Knoll

"That's easy enough for you to say," I remarked. "You're not going to be on the other end of it."

"You're not getting paid enough?" he countered. My bank balance wouldn't be much protection in a hail of AK-47 gunfire from Cuban troops, but I let it drop.

I found the Soviet workmanship very interesting, if dated. Of course, these rifles weren't the newest thing, either. Maybe the best way to describe them is straightforward, not exotic, except for the odd, interesting markings stamped into the metal. The Tokarev, for example, had a star with an arrow inside, something that looked like pi, a K with a circle around it, an E and a triangle. They almost looked like astrological signs, randomly placed, but one probably had to do with manufacturing origin. Maybe the K was Kiev?

"No," Smith said. "It was made in Tula. That's not pi, it's TT. Tokarev from Tula."

How the hell did he know this stuff?

The serial number looked altered, since the numbers were so uneven and hard to read, but maybe that's how they did it. This rifle appeared to be serial number 86689.

The weapons were of better quality than I would have thought, although, in my opinion, not as advanced as the T48. I had tended to think of Russian arms like their clothing: ill-fitted and poorly made, with strings hanging down. The year before, I had played soccer with a guy who had gotten out of Hungary or Poland somehow. He said that, as a kid, he and his little friends used to trail behind the Russian troops and grab the strings that hung down from their overcoats. They would hold the strings as the Russians walked away and the coats would unravel.

The Man on the Grassy Knoll

These weapons would not unravel. I guess their money went somewhere, and it wasn't butter. It must have been guns.

Mr. Smith probably stayed around just for Mrs. Dell's Mexican cooking, because he left shortly after finishing his meal. He said he was going to Tucson, and would check back in three days, which would be about two days too long for me.

I thought Mr. Smith had said the Tokarev also came in a bolt action version, but I had the autoloader. For the job I had to do, I think I would have preferred the former, but maybe Smith was expecting a firefight. That was not an appealing concept. Anyway, I hadn't thought to ask him about this before he took off.

The next morning, Mrs. Dell brought me huevos rancheros, a Mexican omelet laced with picante sauce. My eyes watered, it was so good.

I took the three rifles outside and trudged over to the covered shed, repeating the trip for the ammunition. Smith had told me that all the target paraphernalia was stored in a closed cabinet under a low table. I located it easily enough and sat down on the bench behind the table and set everything up. It was almost nine o'clock in the morning before I was ready. It was already getting hot, even in the shade of the corrugated roof. Unlike in Florida and the Bahamas, I didn't really sweat due to the instant evaporation. My nose was bothering me in the dryness.

Each rifle would be tested at distances from 100 yards up to 400 yards. I knew from experience that I was well within the effective range of the 7.62x.54mmR ammunition, which was about 800 yards. These intervals were already marked on the course. If I still couldn't make up my mind, I'd test other distances, and then the two types of cartridge. Otherwise, I'd wait until I picked the preferred rifle before using the hollow point.

After donning my earmuffs, I began test firing. It was really getting hot and the sunlight was even brighter than it had been in Nassau. Shooting without sunglasses would have been impossible. Mine were expensive and purchased for just this purpose.

I soon judged all three rifles would be adequate for the job. The Tokarev suited me well and felt most comfortable. The rifle seemed to combine the best features of the S.K.S. and the Mosin-Nagant. Smith knew his Soviet weaponry.

Putting aside the other rifles, then, I concentrated on the Tokarev. But it was just too damn hot. I napped, ate Mrs. Dell's enchiladas - delicious, with sour cream - and read until it cooled down. The sun had faded to orange when I resumed with the Tokarev. I practiced until it was just a glow, and then turned on the lights. Mr. Smith was right about the lighting.

In the morning, following another of Mrs. Dell's gourmet omelets - this one with little green peppers and lots of monterey jack cheese - I spent the first hour firing the Tokarev with standard military cartridges. The fully powered rimmed 7.62mm bullet felt heavy like my T48, and the recoil was substantial. I think this was the Russian version of the .308. If I had to fire a second shot, I could lose the target in the scope and have to reacquire it, even using the low-powered 4X instrument. That was the only problem I noted, though, and overall the Tokarev was a competent weapon. My confidence grew with each round, and pretty soon I was very comfortable with the rifle. My accuracy improved close to the T48.

The Man on the Grassy Knoll

I switched ammunition and noted a drop-off in true tracking with the hollow point at the 150 yard target; the trade-off there was obviously the maximum damage this bullet would cause. So it was six of one and a half dozen of the other - distance to target would be the determining factor.

Interestingly, I tried both types on a nearby saguaro. I hated to disfigure this stately guardian of the landscape, but I wanted to see what would happen. Actually, there was very little difference. Mr. Saguaro would never pitch again, but neither cartridge really blasted his arm into kingdom come. I figured the lack of resistance from the pulpy limb inhibited the hollow point from blooming. Over the next two days, I practiced extensively and found I hadn't been supplied with too much ammunition, after all. Disconcertingly, a few of the rounds gave off puffs of white smoke, perhaps due to the age of the ammunition (?). I made a mental note to mention this to Mr. Smith.

By the time he called - there was a phone with no dialer in my trailer - I was totally at ease and quite competent with the Tokarev. I had been asleep to the drone of the air conditioner. He said he would be arriving after supper, so I would have one final hour of practice just to make sure everything was nailed down. I would have told him to come get me even if I wasn't ready - I was itching to get out of that place, Mrs. Dell's cuisine notwithstanding.

Chapter 11

It was now late August or early September. Evidently I wasn't Mr. Smith's only project, and I had been left on my own again for a couple of weeks. I doubted that Smith had teams of marksmen on the loose around the country, but clearly he had other things to do. Still enjoying my expense allowance, I had no objection. I was ensconced in Phoenix, staying at a singles apartment complex off Indian School. There were perhaps a hundred apartments in two buildings, L-shaped affairs situation around a central pool area with exotic landscaping. The buildings were nearly new and the apartments bright, clean and comfortable. I was on a six month lease, as suggested by Mr. Smith.

"Six months?" I had asked.

"So what if you leave early?" he had said. I wondered if anyone else was going to stay in the apartment after I left, and what their business might be.

At night, the soft green lighting shone upward onto the graceful palm trunks and other foliage. It made the entire area seem a showplace. Everything was tasteful. There were probably sixty five women and thirty five guys. No, I had no objection at all.

I had called home pretty regularly, and told my family I was really enjoying my job. That was not a stretch. Everything was fine at home and they wished me well. I had a rented car, an almost new 1963 Ford Galaxie, and was able to explore Phoenix and the surrounding area.   One Sunday, I drove up to the red rock country of Sedona, in the high desert. The beauty was beyond description.   There was a great sense of peace, and one sensed being part of a vast tapestry, where color took the place of speech.

I had asked Mr. Smith if he minded my driving up to Las Vegas for a couple of days, and he said he thought that would be all right, since he wouldn't need me for the following week or so. He cautioned me about avoiding traffic tickets and some of the more colorful attractions of Las Vegas, warning that I could compromise the mission. Smith was sounding like a surrogate father. I was not about to jeopardize my payday, in any event. I had never been to Nevada, and was looking forward to the trip. I was seeing quite a bit of the country on Mr. Smith's expense account, and I thought of my classmates grinding away at what must be dull, uninteresting jobs. Our career choices had seemed unexciting before I met Mr. Smith, and now they appeared totally colorless.

The scenery driving to Las Vegas was awe-inspiring. Strange, gnarled trees, rolling tumbleweeds and the biggest, highest sky I had ever seen. Contrails from jets, so high and white and straight against the deepest blue, soundlessly traced across the sky in a vast geometry. The desert vegetation changed subtly as I drove northward. I saw strange trees with pale green bark and yellow flowers, low cacti strewn across the rocky landscape and clumps of saguaro.   Spines and nettles, lineaments of a harsh world.   I drove out to the Hoover Dam and marveled at the accomplishments of man. Out here, everything was vast, everything was on a bigger plane. The horizon seemed to stretch to forever. A sienna world, where time passed as slowly as the occasional gila monster.

Las Vegas was on a plane of its own. I stayed at the Stardust, took in a number of shows, and learned how quickly one can lose a hundred dollars shooting craps. I decided I liked the town in spite of my lightened wallet, and looked forward to returning after the business with Mr. Smith concluded. If all went well, my bankroll would allow one hell of a week. I wished some of my buddies had been along; things would have been much more fun. I'm not really much of a loner, and I hadn't been with any contemporaries since the week after graduation. I had always had friends and classmates around me, and now my social life was nonexistent. I missed the companionship.

Back in Phoenix, I settled in the furnished apartment. It had a nice kitchen with modern appliances and lots of kitchen implements, many of which baffled me. I wasn't much of a cook. Except for breakfast, I ate out most of the time. Heck, I could afford it. I spent my time reading and exploring the city. It was still desert hot, and the swimming pool was bathtub temperature. At first, I didn't care for it as the water wasn't very refreshing. After a few days, though, I decided I liked it fine. It would be easy to fall asleep in the milk-warm water. After a while, I recognized a few of the regulars, enough to smile and say hello. Invariably, weather was a prime subject of incidental conversation. I noted Phoenicians all seemed to be like the Chamber of Commerce. The weather might be hot, they said, but it was a dry heat. Sure it was. Just like an oven.

I noticed a particularly attractive woman, about my age, tall and willowy. She reminded me of Linda, my teacher friend back at school. Her long blonde hair accented her grace; it seemed to flow about her as she moved. She swam laps most evenings from about 7:30 until 8:00 and seemed in fine shape. When she slipped out of the water, she usually read a magazine or book on one of the chaise lounges. After about a week, I went over and said hello.

Debbie was a marketing trainee for a Phoenix company. She had graduated Arizona State University in Tempe the year before. She was one year older than me. Originally from Glendale, next to Phoenix, she had grown up in the area. I asked her about that.

"Every year, more and more people move out here," she said. "It's getting more crowded and the humidity goes up."

"To what? Eight or nine percent?"

"Sometimes more." She didn't catch my irony.

"Just from people?" I asked. "Do they sweat that much?"

She laughed. It was not unpleasant. Her teeth were very white and even. She also had a knockout figure and a great tan. I decided I liked her pretty much already.

"No, not the people themselves," she said. "The lawns and greenery. They come out here and aren't used to the desert landscape. They don't see the beauty in it, so they plant lots of landscaping and put in grass lawns. Then they have to irrigate. So there is a lot more exposed water, and the humidity goes up around Phoenix. Then all the same people who moved out here because of allergies and asthma and all complain because it's not dry enough." She looked at me, still smiling. "Where are you from?"

The Man on the Grassy Knoll

I would have thought my new career had prepared me for questions like this, but Debbie had me a little flustered. My new phony passport said I was born in New Orleans. I had told Mr. Smith I'd never even been to New Orleans, except for one weekend my junior year, and I didn't remember too much of that. What if somebody asked me something about New Orleans? He had just stared at me.

"Think about that, John. Can you imagine somebody asking you to identify some geographical feature of New Orleans? Proving you were born there? Isn't that pretty unlikely?"

I recall thinking I hoped I'd get better at this. Debbie brought me back to the present.

"Is that a really hard question?" she asked, laughing again. It was soft and musical. Corny, I know. Boy, was I getting dopey.

"Oh, no. No." I finally piped up. "I know where I'm from. I'm from upstate New York." I had been there once, as a kid in summertime, to Penn Yan, Watkins Glen and Dundee. The Finger Lakes were beautiful and I had fond memories. I could fake it if she knew the area.

"I've never been there," she said. "I've never been east of the Rockies." She smiled again. We chatted on and that's when I found out Debbie was a marketing trainee. Mr. Smith's cover story about a government job had only extended to my parents, and a few friends who had asked, but the story was serviceable enough for Debbie. I was glad my first name was still John.

We agreed to meet by the pool again the next evening. It was really enjoyable. We found we shared many of the same interests, although I declined to mention shooting, carrying false identification, or planning to take out Fidel Castro. On the next Friday night, I took Debbie to dinner and splurged at the Camelback Inn, courtesy of Mr. Smith.

If she looked good poolside, she was a vision by candlelight. The flickering flame played with the highlights of her hair, sparkled her eyes. I know how dumb that sounds, but that's what I thought. I felt myself getting stupid again and enjoying it. It struck me that Debbie and Mirasol, both beautiful and feminine, were polar opposites: Debbie was liquid sunshine, cheerful and open, Mirasol the cool tropical night, with a promise of mysterious secrets. I still thought of Mirasol from time to time, still wondered what had happened to her and her brother.

Maybe more than just from time to time.

"I've been here for a couple of special occasions growing up," Debbie said, looking around as she sipped a White Russian. "It's a wonderful place."

It sure seemed wonderful to me, I thought, gulping my Bloody Mary. I wanted another right away but didn't want to appear an alcoholic. I asked Debbie about her job and had no idea what she said. I snapped out of my reverie when she asked a question.

"What?" I blurted.

"I asked if you always were an outdoorsman, if that's why you went with the Forest Service."

Is that what I'd said? I didn't remember, exactly. I was going to have to be more careful.

"Aah, yeah – yes. Outdoors. I've always hiked and enjoyed the woods and all," I heard myself say. What? I'd never hiked in my life except maybe once. When I was about nine, my dad had taken me camping with the neighbors. We'd gotten lost trying to find a stream.

"Plus playing sports. I played varsity baseball in college." I wanted to impress her, but I figured I'd better leave out hunting and target shooting.

We ordered chateaubriand with a white wine reduction and shallots moistened with demi-glace. I really didn't know what the hell it was but I had tried to sound sophisticated as I perused the menu and made the suggestion. It proved a wonderful choice, actually. The meal fit in with the whole evening, which seemed to float along like a cloud. Debbie must have remembered my remark about hiking, because the next evening she suggested that Saturday we clamber up a mountain called Pinnacle Peak in nearby Scottsdale. We did, and were rewarded by visiting a restaurant where we ate mesquite-fired steak and cowboy beans.

Debbie was a real sweetheart and I enjoyed her company very much. She was intelligent but didn't complicate things, like most women. She was always in an upbeat mood. I had the presence of mind to tell her, pretty much up front, that I would not be staying long in Phoenix. We spent several evenings together and I reflected on how life seemed to run like an old river, full of meanderings and unexpected turns, on its inexorable course downstream. I knew our dalliance would be short-lived, as indeed it was, but if I had had a regular job in Arizona there would have been a lot more to our relationship. But then again, I hadn't had much luck getting a regular job.

Chapter 12

Mr. Smith came to Phoenix shortly after Labor Day. I picked him up at Sky Harbor Airport and we drove out to the resort area. I asked him how everything was going. How was Mrs. Dell?

"Everything's in good shape. Mrs. Dell is doing just fine, I'm sure. We've got a lot to discuss after dinner."

Smith checked into the Arizona Biltmore. Lovely. It was luxurious enough for me to wonder if this was totally on the government's tab. It seemed his budget constraints fell outside the normal limits. He checked in under the name Conway, or Conroy. He had only the one bag. He went to his room while I wandered around the lobby. After he had freshened up, he rejoined me and we went into the dining room.

Since The Last Concert Café and Mrs. Dell's huevos rancheros and enchiladas, I had developed quite a taste for Mexican food. The Biltmore's fare was superb: the cheese and onion enchiladas were light and delicious, the black beans juicy and flavorful. The salsa was just spicy enough. Our conversation was pleasant and light. Life was constantly improving. I couldn't say I'd become comfortable with the mission, but rather reconciled to it, and felt confident I could do the job when the time came.

The Man on the Grassy Knoll

Later, we walked through the grounds to Smith's room. Very nice indeed. Colored spotlight at the bases of the palm trees created an atmosphere of natural beauty. Lighting, in Phoenix, was as much an accent to decorating as furniture. We both sat around a table in the corner, relaxing in the comfortable, overstuffed armchairs. Outside the window, palm fronds rustled in a light breeze, highlighted in greens and blues.

"Think you've gotten a little rusty with the Tokarev?" Mr. Smith asked.

"No, but I'd like one session with the rifle before the mission, though. Just to make sure. Do you have any idea when that is going to happen?"

"Well, that's part of what I need to talk to you about," he said. "I want to address the overall picture. John, you've done well so far. I knew you would when we picked you out. We're very pleased."

Pleased with what? I hadn't done much of anything lately, unless we counted Debbie, or losing a hundred bucks in Las Vegas, and I'm sure he hadn't meant either of those. He continued.

"When we began, I spoke to you about the grave threat posed by that madman in Havana. Do you remember that?"

"Sure," I said. How could I forget what this whole thing was about?

"We've come to the conclusion that Mr. Castro is a manifestation of the problem, and a thorn in our side, but he is not the central problem. He is not the larger problem."

He paused. Mr. Smith was now choosing his words carefully. Was the mission over? Maybe he was he going to fire me from my first job. Did he want the money back?

"Let me give you a larger perspective. What do you know about the missile crisis and the Bay of Pigs invasion?"

"Just what I read in the papers, but I was pretty busy back then." Studying, sports, carousing, drinking, carrying on.

"Do you know we trained an invasion force of well over a thousand troops, fourteen hundred freedom fighters, to invade the south coast of Cuba in 1961?"

I hadn't known the Bay of Pigs was in the south, I remember thinking. Not that it made much difference. Did they ride around the island first?

"President John Kennedy approved the invasion plan. That is no secret. The United States was supposed to provide air cover and other support for the invasion force. But we didn't."

"We didn't?" Had I known that? Yes, I knew that. I couldn't remember, exactly.

"No, we didn't. Kennedy pulled the plug on Zapata."

"What's Zapata?" I asked.

"Oh. That's the mission code name. Everything has a code name, don't you read the spy novels? Oh yes, you do read about mercury bullets, don't you? Anyway, the President deliberately canceled the air cover and other support. He let the troops land anyway, knowing the whole mission was now hopeless. Castro's troops met them on the beach. The Cuban soldiers were already in position, because they had been tipped off. The invasion failed, the men were cut to pieces or captured, and the whole thing was a disaster. The troops that weren't killed were imprisoned and later most of them were ransomed out."

"Why?" I was a college graduate with good grades. I suppose I should have known why.

The Man on the Grassy Knoll

"And, Kennedy took out a potential roadblock to his longer-range plans with disinformation. Adlai Stevenson was left to make a joke out of himself at the UN. Kennedy made sure of that."

"Why?" I repeated.

"Stevenson's agenda was for detente."

"What are you talking about?"

"In 1962, Kennedy brought us to the brink of nuclear war with his Cuban missile confrontation."

"Wait a minute," I said. "He couldn't allow those missiles to stay in Cuba. What are you saying?"

"Then why are they still there?"

"What? They're not there. What do you mean?" I stammered.

"Just what I said. Some missiles are *still there.*"

"No they're not. They took the missiles out. They photographed them on the ship's decks."

"Did they? Ever see a missile leave Cuba? You watched the news, didn't you? What did you see?"

"I saw missiles leave Cuba on Russian ships," I said.

"Not entirely. Sometimes you saw shots of tarpaulins covering cylindrical shapes of what were supposed to look like missiles up on deck. You saw crates. But you didn't see any missiles."

"Actually, I wouldn't know what was a real missile, exactly," I said. "Are you saying those were props? That stuff was fake?"

"Some of them. Enough of them. We showed the President beyond question that a significant number of missiles were still on Cuban soil, and they still *are* on Cuban soil.

Many of those crates were empty. The tarps covered wooden framing and curved sheet metal. Mock-ups."

I cocked my head. "Come on."

"Want to know the easiest way to prove it? Look at the pictures of the ships steaming out of Havana harbor. Look at their waterlines. Missiles and launchers and support pieces are heavy. Some of those ships are riding at a high load line. They aren't carrying anything."

I didn't recall ever seeing pictures of the ships steaming out of Havana, except looking straight down to the decks.

Smith continued. "We showed President Kennedy everything I'm telling you and a lot more I'm not. There was no doubt the Soviets double-crossed us. *No doubt.* Yet Kennedy did nothing."

This was all shocking news. Was it true? How could he tell me this if it wasn't?

"Can you show me these ship pictures and the waterlines?" I asked.

"Sure. You'll see for yourself."

"Then why didn't everyone see it?"

"Some of these pictures are classified," Smith said. "The telltale shots were withheld from publication."

I really didn't know where ships' waterlines were supposed to be.

"Are you wondering why he did nothing?"

I supposed I was. I was still a little behind, though. As I said, this was boggling my mind.

"Do you remember 1960? Right after Kennedy took office?"

"What?" Had Kennedy given away nuclear secrets?

The Man on the Grassy Knoll

"Communist troops invaded Laos and were threatening South Vietnam. We had a commitment to stop them. Instead, Kennedy started the Peace Corps. Think they were handy with the Tokarev?"

"Well...," was all I could manage to say.

"There's more, but I'm just hitting the highlights. The new test-ban treaty. Stops *us* from testing, anyway."

He stopped talking for awhile. I didn't know what to think.

"Any of this stuff, feel free to check out for yourself. Think about the questions. Why? Why?"

"Okay. Why?"

"Think about Kennedy's background. Wealthy family. Social giveaway programs. Classic rich man's guilt. Communism, Socialism, in their purest form. What do they promise?"

"You're saying the President of the United States is a traitor?" I asked, incredulous. "A subversive?"

"Priorities have changed. You've got a new target."

Chapter 13

I gasped in disbelief. This was not happening. *Shoot the President of the United States?* This was insanity. In a moment, Smith would break into laughter. He couldn't be serious.

But of course he was. Suddenly, this grand adventure had turned into – what?

I shook my head. "No. No. No way. Even if everything you say is true, I'm out. Forget it. The hell with this. Forget it. Get some Special Forces guy or something. Find some other sharpshooter who thinks like you do. Who the hell am I, John Wilkes Booth? Sic semper tyrannis?"

Smith said nothing. A minute or two went by. I was still shaking my head. My legs were shaking, too. My heavy breathing was the only sound in the room; I couldn't seem to slow it down. More time went by. I looked at Smith; he was expressionless. Presently I got up and looked out the window. In the clear, dry air there were a zillion stars upstairs.

Boy, I thought my life had turned upside down before. I didn't know the half of it. Now it's inside out.

And then:

I've got to get the hell away from this madman. I've got to get out of here.

85

The Man on the Grassy Knoll

Outside, the fronds rustled like before. Amazing. It was all so peaceful, so pretty. Outside the window, nothing had changed.

I came back and sat down opposite Mr. Smith. I got control of my breathing as I realized what a dupe I'd been.

"You knew this all the time, didn't you? All along. Castro wasn't the target. I don't even remember you actually *saying* Castro was the target. Not that it would have mattered. It wouldn't have mattered anyway. You thought I'm just a patsy. Some jerkwater English major with the ink still wet on his diploma." I rambled on like that until I petered out. There was a silence as I just shook my head back and forth.

Mr. Smith finally spoke. "No, John, we didn't trick you. You're definitely not a patsy. A patsy is somebody you leave holding the bag, like Stevenson. Our vital concern has always been your safety and the ability to get away."

"So you wouldn't get caught."

"We could have ensured your silence anyway," he said. Boy, I didn't like the implications of that. "But regardless of what you may think at the moment, we are loyal Americans who believe in the freedoms and justice system this country is based on. John, if you firmly believed someone in the highest position of authority in the land was working very hard to bring about the downfall of all you believe in, wouldn't you come to the same decision? Is it easier to shoot a man on the battlefield who doesn't hate you and only wants to go home?"

"He may not hate me but he's got a gun and he's trying to kill me," I said. I paused. "All I ever wanted to do is play baseball for a living. Maybe be a writer. I didn't ask for any of this."

The Man on the Grassy Knoll

"It would be nice if the pen were mightier than the sword. Then maybe I wouldn't have a job. Listen, what you said is true. But who ever asks for it? The private in the foxhole ordered over the top? You must have read *All Quiet on the Western Front? Johnny Got His Gun*?"

In fact, I had read Dalton Trumbo's shocking anti-war novel.

Smith continued. "John, do you remember those German generals who tried to stop Adolf Hitler and end the war? Do you remember reading about that?"

My chair was not that comfortable anymore. I shifted my position.

"I remember." They'd planted a bomb in the room where Hitler met with his generals. We'd read about it in high school. It didn't seem too real, then. It was just history.

"Were they traitors? Were they castigated? No, they were heroes, weren't they?"

"All the way to the firing squad," I said.

"They died with their heads held high. They did the best they could. They had no choice but to risk their lives to save their people."

"You're talking to me about dying? What the hell interest do I have in dying?!" My voice had risen about two octaves. "You do it, if you want to die. I've got my whole life ahead of me. Don't talk to me about dying, for Chrissake. Get the goddamn Marines."

I don't know why, but all of a sudden I felt like all the air had been let out of me. I wasn't even that mad at Mr. Smith.

"What a dope I've been. I guess you figured I was easy pickings for professionals like you."

"John, we can't make you do anything you don't want to do. You know that. And I wasn't trying to threaten you before. You can still bow out of this."

I looked closely at Smith. For the first time, I didn't believe him. I was starting to feel tendrils of panic around my insides.

"We are also prepared to adjust the financial aspect of this project," he said.

More money? I thought for a few seconds. What did that mean? If they were going give me a raise, then I was even more valuable to them, and maybe not so readily expendable. Maybe.

"What do you mean?"

"We are prepared to pay you $150,000 to help us. Another forty five thousand now, in your account. And the balance upon completion. Be comforted in the thought that the highest levels of national security are behind you, counting on you. We must save this country."

A hundred and fifty thousand dollars?! This was beyond serious money. This was even more than the Yankees paid Mickey Mantle. Smith and his people - apparently the highest levels of national security - certainly had the strength of their convictions. They were all behind me, it seemed. How dangerous was this guy in the White House? Was our whole way of life at risk? Maybe it really was. Somebody was betting a fortune on it.

I could retire on that kind of money, and I had just started. Still...

"Judas took thirty pieces of silver."

"Judas betrayed the Son of God," countered Smith. "John Kennedy is the son of Joseph Kennedy."

Chapter 14

The human mind can trip like a circuit breaker. When something is so terrible, so nearly beyond contemplation, defense mechanisms spring up to protect the psyche. I think that's what happened to me. I was in way over my head now. I had two nightmarish choices, it seemed: go along with the plan, or risk getting killed if I backed out. Smith had hinted as much.

Sure, I wanted the money, whosoever it was. I didn't come from a rich family; my dad worked very hard to send me to college. My discouraging experience with job interviews had left me feeling out of step with my peers. I hadn't really wanted to get hired, and I hadn't been hired. My sports career was over. I wasn't going to law school, at least this year. What the hell was I going to do, teach English in high school somewhere? This was all pretty scary. A hundred and fifty thousand dollars fixed a lot of things, all right.

But money wasn't enough. It would never be a compelling reason. Not for something like this. I wasn't a contract hit man, for Chrissake.

I mulled over the things Smith had said. He had intimated that others in the intelligence community, those in high places, regarded Kennedy as someone who must be stopped. I went to the library and reviewed the Bay of Pigs invasion material, and the articles about the Cuban missile withdrawal. It was true; Kennedy had pulled the air cover at the Bay of Pigs. What the hell sense did that make? I couldn't find much about the ships that carried the missiles, except that they were Soviet warships and the goods were supposed to be visible on deck. So why would Kennedy let them use tarpaulins? That made no sense either. I made another mental note to make sure Smith got me those photos. I might not be able to interpret them correctly, without having the expertise, but I could at least try to find out he had any pictures at all.

I brought myself up to date on President Kennedy's administration. By the fall of 1963, the President's popularity had waned. Critical failings, as outlined by Mr. Smith, had taken the luster off the Kennedy presidency. The Democratic Party was in trouble. Mr. Smith was suggesting that the failings of the administration were largely deliberate, at best reckless.

It was hard to know what to think. I had no one to talk to, to exchange thoughts with, to bounce ideas off. I was on my own. If I had any chance of reaching a logical conclusion, I needed to push emotion out of the equation, at least for the time being. Feelings needed to be put aside or I'd never figure anything out. I sat alone at a long library table, surrounded by old issues of Time and other periodicals I'd perused. No one was near me. Sunlight slanted through the stained glass window and painted colors across the table.

I'd gotten good grades all through college. I needed to treat this like a textbook problem. I took a deep breath, clearing my mind.

So okay, what could I deduce? I'd researched everything I could find. Yes, the Bay of Pigs had been a horrendous failure. There had been, clearly, many mistakes by the young President's regime but mistakes alone did not warrant extreme action. All Presidents made mistakes. The question was whether or not these actions were part of a deliberate course of action designed with another agenda in mind. It seemed to come down to Smith's argument about the missile crisis. There appeared no logical explanation for Kennedy's handling of the missile removal, if indeed he knew the Russians had cheated. Against the backdrop of JFK's pulling the air cover from the Bay of Pigs invasion and causing a disastrous defeat, it would appear damning evidence.

That meant the pictures of the Russian ships would be a critical issue for me. If Smith could show me those ships were carrying dummy cargo, then I had to assume someone had shown those pictures to the President, whether from Smith's agency or the military or whomever. That's all, I said to myself, I can do. I had no way of verifying most of his other allegations, anyway.

It took Mr. Smith about ten days to procure the photos of the Russian fleet exiting Cuba. We met at a Chinese restaurant, of all places: the Sing High, which was over on Madison, I think. Kind of a dumpy part of Phoenix - I wondered how he knew about the place. It turned out we both had a fondness for wonton soup, egg rolls, and shrimp with lobster sauce. We had a contest to see who could eat an egg roll with the most Chinese mustard, and I won. Hours later, when I regretted the dumb match, I recalled my dad and I had done the same thing when I was in high school. What a slow learner.

After the shrimp with lobster sauce, fortune cookies, and ice cream, Smith pulled out one of his manila envelopes. The restaurant was nearly deserted and no one at all was nearby. The lighting was not good but Smith produced a small flashlight.

The pictures were quite large, perhaps 8" x 10". They were glossy black and whites. Most appeared to have been taken from an altitude of a few hundred feet, and these were shot from the side. Some had scale markings along the margin.

"Who took these?" I inquired.

"The Navy was in charge of the verification operation. But everybody wanted to get involved."

"Explain these to me."

"These photographs were taken at various distances from the Russian vessels, at altitudes up to several hundred feet after they steamed out of Havana. Most were taken while the ships were within 50 miles of Cuba. We have more pictures, at different altitudes and attitudes, but these are the ones you need to see. Hold the flashlight while I show you what's important."

I held the little light for him. It was very powerful and the beam was concentrated, but it created a glare. Smith pulled out a pen to use as a pointer.

A waiter approached. Smith took back the flashlight and switched it off, scooping the pictures upside down in his lap. The waiter dropped off the check. After he left, Smith switched the flashlight back on and brought the pictures back up on the table. Idly, I noticed the back of the bottom picture was resting on some rice covered with sticky lobster sauce. Smith must not have noticed. There wasn't a lot of room to spread out the photos, and the table wasn't too well-lit. I was glad he brought the light.

The Man on the Grassy Knoll

"Look at the waterlines. Look at how far into the water these ships are riding. Riding pretty high, aren't they?"

How the hell did I know? I couldn't tell anything from the pictures. One showed two or three ships and something else. I couldn't make out what it was.

"What's this thing?" I asked. Whatever it was looked out of focus.

Smith just looked at me, a half-smile on his face.

"You don't know what that is?" he asked. "It's an airplane, for Chrissake. It's one of ours that got in the picture. Can't you tell an airplane? How the hell do you shoot straight if you can't see that?" Smith was amused. I could tell. "I told you everybody wanted to get involved. They were all tripping over each other."

"Well, it's kind of hard to see in here. That light makes a glare, anyway," I responded, defensively. Something was ringing a bell. "Don't ships have markings on the side to tell how far up or down they're riding? What the limits are?"

"Sure, cargo vessels and tankers do. But these are warships, not commercial vessels. They don't have those markings. But we still can tell."

From the envelope, Smith extracted a second set of photos. They looked almost exactly the same.

"What is this? It's the same thing."

"Is it?" Smith said, smiling. "Turn them over." I did so. "Look at the dates. Now look at the dates on the backs of the first set I showed you."

The second set of pictures showed a whole bunch of earlier dates. Some were within a couple of weeks of the first pictures, and some were much earlier. When I turned over the first set, wet sticky rice fell in my lap. I didn't get it.

The Man on the Grassy Knoll

"I don't get it," I said.

"Simple," said Smith. "We wanted to make sure those ships left with what they were supposed to leave with. So we photographed a couple of them on the way in, when they were carrying nothing. Others are file photos. Look at where they're riding."

"Where?" I asked.

"There's no difference at all."

I squinted at both sets. I couldn't tell anything except that the water was choppy in most of the pictures.

"I really can't tell anything from these, to tell you the truth. I'm still going to have to take this on faith, if I take it at all."

"The entire U.S. population took it on faith when the first pictures were released. Do you think they could tell anything from any of them? Of course not. They had to take it on faith, just like you."

"But they were wrong."

"Because the news was managed and they didn't see these. Nor had you until today."

I wanted to ask Smith about something I'd read when I looked this stuff up. "I thought the U.N. was supposed to supervise the dismantling and loading of the missiles and loaders and their sites."

"Never happened. Kennedy backed down. It was ludicrous. I'll even give you specifics. There were sites scattered all over Cuba. Many places had multiple installations. Guanajay had three Intermediate Range Ballistic Missile sites. The Russians played the old shell game, and only two actually got loaded."

I concentrated on committing the site names to memory. I didn't know if I could ever check up on Mr. Smith's story, but at least I could try. He continued.

"San Cristobal and Sagua La Grande were multiple Medium Range sites. They only loaded half the missiles. Remember, the pictures of the ships were only one source of information for us. We had confirmation on the ground for what I'm telling you."

"From who?" I interrupted.

"Someone who would know."

"Come on, you've got to give me more than that. What's his name? What's he do?"

Smith looked at me, hesitated for a second. "He's a Russian colonel. We call him Ollie. Forget I said that. Think, now. If you take out 75% of half the firepower of World War II, and leave 25%, you still accomplished your goal, didn't you?"

"What's left is 25% of all of World War II firepower?" I asked, incredulous.

"12 ½%. You're supposed to be a college graduate. I guess English majors don't have to know math. No. But I'm making a point."

"Didn't we do a head count? Didn't we know how many missiles were involved?"

"Listen, John. The Soviets were supposed to pull back the tarpaulins for the Navy to verify the missile count. Sometimes they only pulled back a corner and that's where they had the dummy sheet metal, all mocked up like an actual missile. Sometimes they didn't even do that. They only needed a small area to look like the real thing. They were looking ship to ship, anyway, so what the hell could they really see?"

I looked again at the pictures. "How can anyone really tell what they're looking at? What are these, model rockets? I can't tell anything."

"You're looking at small black and white glossies. We look at positives, like acetates, backlit and blown up much bigger. We have people trained on nothing but stuff like this. It's their life's work. Can you read an x-ray? Looks incomprehensible to you and me. But your doctor can."

"Has President Kennedy seen these?"

Smith looked pained. "What do you think?"

"What did he say?"

"I wasn't there. I was told he didn't say much of anything. He overruled his security advisors and took no action at all."

I looked one more time at the pictures. "Are you sure the missiles and their support stuff are that heavy? How can I find that out?"

"Probably look it up in Jane's, I imagine," said Smith. "But ask yourself this question. Why would we go to all the time, trouble, and maybe risk to get these pictures if we couldn't tell anything from them?"

I asked myself that question. Even without the $150,000 issue, I was alarmed.

By now, there was only one other couple in the place. I supposed Mr. Smith had a cast iron bladder, because he was still sipping tea. I couldn't stand the stuff. He seemed to be weighing something in his mind.

"Okay, look," he said. "I'll tell you something nobody knows about, so you'll understand what I'm really trying to tell you. There are six tactical nuclear missile weapons still in Cuba that we had no idea existed. They have nothing to do with the other IRBM's and MRBM's. We only found out by accident. The really bad part about this is that they were under local control, so that Moscow couldn't stop them from being used. When all the debate was going on at the ExComm - that's Kennedy's Executive Committee that worked on the crisis - there were a lot of votes to invade Cuba, as you might imagine. What nobody knew is that the local command had these tactical missiles ready to fire at the beaches after we would have landed. It would have wiped out the entire invasion force and started World War III. What happened was that we got a frantic phone call from Petrov- from our Soviet Colonel mole telling us about the six weapons out of Moscow's control. A goddamn ordinary phone call. Can you imagine? How lucky we were the call went through and got answered?"

Smith let this percolate down. My God.

"Those six weapons are still there. You liked Miami, didn't you? Know how long it would take one of them to get downtown?"

A surreal picture of some Russian rocket taking a supersonic header into the Fontainebleau swimming pool, with a Cyrillic greeting from the Kremlin written on the side, flashed through my mind. What a nightmare.

Everybody out of the pool.

"Look, there's a lot more but I can't tell you everything," Smith continued. "Do you know Khrushchev offered to take the missiles out of Cuba if we would take our Jupiter IRBMs out of Turkey, right on their back door?"

The Man on the Grassy Knoll

"I don't know if I knew it or not." My mind was spinning. I was getting a headache. "IRBM?"

"Intermediate Range Ballistic Missile. Kennedy didn't want them out of there yet. Know why?"

Of course I didn't know why. "Because he's really a loyal American democrat?"

"Close. He's a Democrat, all right, because an election year's right around the corner. The reason was mostly partisan politics - re-election at all costs. If Kennedy yanked the Jupiters out of Turkey, he wouldn't have a big political victory, just a stand-off. Also, he wanted to piss Khrushchev off, and he succeeded. He provoked him into cheating on the withdrawal. The whole thing was cooked up mostly by Bobby Kennedy, anyway. Besides, the Jupiters couldn't hit a barn door, they're so unreliable. They were more dangerous to Turkey than to Russia. Didn't know that, did you? They couldn't get out of their own way. They were expensive window dressing. Khrushchev isn't as smart as Kennedy. The Jupiters were coming out regardless, in a couple of months - think about that. So he just ignored Khrushchev's request, and told him to get the missiles out of Cuba anyway. Against McNamara's advice. A game within a game. But the Russian was too dumb to figure it out. Remember, he's from peasant stock. Kennedy just couldn't call him up and explain, even if he wanted to. What the hell, until recently, they could hardly communicate at all, anyway. The Russians had to talk to Kennedy on Radio Moscow. So anyway Khrushchev reneged on the withdrawal. Like I said, Kennedy wanted to piss him off so maybe he'd keep a few megatons around the Havana Hilton or trigger some other confrontational event short of a nuclear response. It worked only too well. But Khrushchev didn't know Kennedy would know, or that if he did he wouldn't do anything about it."

This was confusing. I tried to follow. I was having a hard time.

"Actually, do you want to know how dumb Khrushchev is, anyway?" Smith asked, after a pause.

"Sure, I guess."

"Khrushchev actually sent two letters to Kennedy. The second one was a committee letter. They only thought up the idea to trade off the Jupiters for the Cuban missiles after Khrushchev had sent the first letter, offering to withdraw if only we promised not to invade Cuba. It's so dumb it would be laughable if this moron didn't have his ham hock on the big button. It's even dumber than that because Bobby Kennedy had planted the idea with the Russians that we might take the Jupiters out of Turkey and maybe Italy. He helped their thinking process along, partly so Kennedy could turn them down later, and piss them off, and partly because of his real agenda. Either way he figured he'd win. Do you see why all this is so dangerous? Why someday you could be walking down the street on a beautiful spring morning with your wife and kids, on your way to church or a ball game, and all of a sudden the sky lights up so bright it's like a million suns and the next instant you're not even a thought? And you had no idea why or that there was even anything going on? Do you now see how dangerous all these games are? And Kennedy thinks he's entitled to play them, like some kind of high stakes teeter-totter, because he thinks Khrushchev won't go to war. Kennedy's ratings shoot way back up. The pot keeps simmering, but not quite boiling over and he thinks he can control it. But he didn't know about that little six pack surprise in Cuba, did he? Kind of a major megaton miscalculation. It's just a big goddamn Harvard intellectual football game. With the nuclear football. So he shoves aside thoughtful men like Stevenson who try and use intelligence and reasonable judgment."

Smith could talk like that sometimes. He really could. If someone else said the same words, they'd come out forced, said for effect. When Smith spoke them, they were convincing. You wanted to believe the guy; he had that gift. Ironically, I thought, he'd have had a great career in politics.

He paused for a moment. When he continued, his voice was subdued. "You see, it doesn't even matter if Kennedy's a Socialist or Communist or even a Whig. He's far more dangerous than Khrushchev, because Khrushchev doesn't really want war, never mind the field commanders. Kennedy's an incalculably dangerous threat to the entire world."

There was a long silence. I tried to assimilate all that Smith had said, despite all his mixed metaphors. I had never heard him so impassioned; he was a cool customer but if he was acting now he was sure fooling me.

"Did you work for Stevenson?" I asked, finally.

Smith looked pained. "Give me some credit. Nobody worked for Stevenson. He's just an example."

"Does Khrushchev know about Kennedy?" I asked.

"Of course not," was the reply.

Smith drove the arrow home. "Ask yourself another question: what possible legitimate reason could Kennedy have for ignoring these pictures?"

I couldn't think of one.

Smith let me chew on that for awhile. Then he spoke again.

"Ask yourself another question: why wouldn't Kennedy withdraw the Jupiter missiles, and defuse the situation, when he knew they were coming out of Turkey anyway? Why would he deliberately provoke the Russians, against the advice of his own Secretary of Defense?"

"How do you know they're going to come out of Turkey?" I asked.

"They're already gone. Why did he criticize this year's Cuban rebel attacks in the press? Whose side is he on? *Who tipped off the Cuban troops at Playa Giron?"*

Playa Giron?!?

His words were a jolt of electricity.

"The invasion was at Playa Giron? The Bay of Pigs?"

Smith nodded. "The main invasion, yes."

"What was the date?" I asked. I had a strong sense of foreboding.

"April 17, 1961."

Chapter 15

Smith was looking at me closely. I realized my mouth was open.

"What?" he asked.

"Can you get me a list of the Cuban exiles who participated in the Bay of Pigs invasion?" I asked.

"That's an awfully big list. Why?"

"I need to know about two names. I need to know about Ramon Figueroa and Abelardo Figueroa."

"Why?"

"You said some were executed and the rest ransomed out."

"Not all of them. They captured maybe twelve hundred Brigade 2506 members. Some went to prison. Several hundred were executed, including a few U.S. citizens. Most were ransomed out for a bunch of farm tractors and other stuff. A bunch were K.I.A."

"I need to know what happened to Ramon and Abelardo, his father. I need to know if they were in the landing party that got wiped out because Kennedy yanked the air cover."

"I might be able to do that. Who are they to you?"

"Ramon was my freshman roommate and a fraternity brother. My best friend. He was another pitcher on the baseball team. Abelardo was his father. They fled Cuba in 1959, I think. They're from Playa Giron."

"What makes you think they participated?"

"Ramon disappeared from school in March, a month before the invasion. His father came up to school and met with him. Ramon knows his way around weapons. And it was their home town, for Chrissake."

Ramon and Abelardo were huddled under a tree, in some intense conversation. . .

Smith looked thoughtful. "I'll see what I can find out."

"If I do this – this thing, this - if there's a change in administrations, I want to know what's going to happen with Cuba." For some reason, I couldn't think of the name of the current vice president. I was pretty upset.

"Well, it couldn't get worse, could it? Every effort would be made to ease tensions, normalize relations. That's the whole point. I'll promise you this. If your people were involved, I'll find out what happened to them. If they're in prison, we'll do what we can to get them released."

Later, I sat out by the pool in my apartment complex and thought. It was quite late and I was alone with the palms and little waterfall. The sound of the water was soothing but I was wide awake, my mind running in high gear.

There appeared little doubt my friend and possibly his father had been involved in the doomed invasion. I desperately wished to find Mirasol, who must have anguished about her brother and father, and would be able to verify where they'd gone, what they'd done, maybe what had happened to them. They must have told her, or she would have known, that it was all top secret and that's probably why she never contacted me. The irony was stupefying, it was infuriating: a tragedy made even more tragic, considering what I was hired to do. I could have popped a filling grinding my teeth.

And all because of politics. Nuclear politics. Politics or something more sinister, as Smith was claiming. He seemed to be right; it really didn't matter why.

Smith had told me the highest levels of our national security were counting on me. They had the wherewithal to pay me a fortune to accomplish what they and Smith believed needed to be done. It certainly appeared Kennedy's agenda was dangerous at best, treacherous at worst. And now it had gotten personal, most likely. I could think of no other explanation for the sudden disappearance of the Figueroas.

Someone had to do it, it seemed.

Someone outside the normal channels of command, answerable to no one. Someone free from personal responsibilities, able to move and act for months without accountability, isolated from government and therefore insulated against all possible leaks. Like a spore, floating free, protected, ready to alight and spring into action.

Someone who could shoot straight.

Someone who was going to get the $150,000, because Smith was determined to get the job done. The universe of possible candidates, I was realizing, might have been quite limited when Smith started his search. The military would have been off-limits. Nonetheless, if I backed out now, he would doubtless find another recruit. I would become a liability. A risk. If I didn't believe him, and tried to alert the authorities to stop him, he would vanish. But I wouldn't disappear, at least not voluntarily. I'd be around, and he could find me, with John Graves' identification or my own. It might not just be my phony ID that had a limited life. I was sure he could freeze the $30,000 in Nassau, and maybe now I knew why he had me open the account in my real name - there was no way to explain that away. I was painted into a corner, and Mr. Smith had given me the brush.

I needed to get back and write down everything Smith had told me, concentrate on every detail I could remember, in case I needed to document things later. I had to look at a map and try to find the site names he had rattled off, and match them up with real places in Cuba. Somehow, I felt I might need to do that. So I did.

The thing was, though, I did believe him.

Mr. Smith needed someone, and he needed him soon.

But not me.

Chapter 16

No, not me. No way. I didn't need this. I sure as hell didn't ask for this. Fidel, that was one thing. It had taken me a couple of months to come to grips with that operation. But this? Certainly not until I knew about my best friend, and that would be up to Mr. Smith. The ball was in his court now. Until then, not me.

Then who?

How the hell would I know? I was as patriotic as the next guy, I suppose. It made sense intellectually, and maybe even on a gut level, but there was no way I could do the work. Could I?

And what if Smith couldn't find anyone? What then?

I thought about the bullshit macho games they were playing in the White House, and how they'd already backfired big time, and it hadn't made those guys blink. And I got scared. I thought about my mom and dad, eating supper one night maybe, and all of a sudden, just like Smith had said, somebody in Russia turns on the klieg lights and vaporizes them and all my teammates and fraternity brothers, and Linda, my teacher girlfriend with the dreamy smile who cooked those terrific liver and onion dinners, and Debbie, with her freckles and warm laugh, and Mirasol, with the dark, smoldering eyes who I had kissed and held so briefly, and all the little kids running around, a few of which I knew, little cousins and relatives and all, now just shadows on the sidewalk, if they're lucky, and if they're not, they wind up looking all melted like those Hiroshima victims who had the misfortune to live. And I thought if that happened, and I could have stopped those madmen in the White House, what then? Would I be like the guy who sees an accident and doesn't stop to help? No, I would be worse, because I could have prevented it. Maybe I'd be closer to a mass murderer. Smith had opened my eyes, no matter how tightly I had wanted to squeeze them shut, and showed me what people didn't want to know and wouldn't believe anyway.

I had little doubt he'd told the truth. That was my judgment. He'd had the goods, shown me the pictures, provided details. I'd researched his claims in the library, spent hours perusing periodicals, newspapers, journals. I couldn't verify much, of course, but whatever I did learn matched up. Once I believed his story, it followed that the Kennedys needed to be stopped. If it had to be me, if this terrible job fell to me, for whatever reason, maybe call it fate, maybe call it bad luck, then the trick would be to commit once and for all to this drastic course of action and not think about it anymore. It would be corny to call it a higher calling, a patriotic act, a noble sacrifice. Cold comfort if I were caught, or failed, and even if we pulled it off. I realized my life would be forever altered, should I go through with this. Hell, it could be ended.

Would I be emotionally damaged? Or was I mollycoddling myself to think so? After all, a whole generation, my father and a couple of uncles included, fought for our country and killed people with guns and bayonets and grenades and mortars and all kinds of weapons. They didn't seem too emotionally damaged. They put down their guns and came back and picked up their plows, or machine tools, or whatever, and went to work building America strong. And then they put all that stuff down and dusted off their M1s and did it all over again in Korea. And maybe it was harder for them, because picking off some zipperhead on a Pacific island or some gook running down Pork Chop Hill might not exactly relate to saving the homeland, whereas my action could directly protect all my fellow citizens. Yeah, I was young, but so were they, for Chrissake. Some were four or five years younger than I or more, the ones who lied to get into the action. I wouldn't have to eat c-rations or freeze my ass off at the Chosin Reservoir or in the Ardennes or anything, not leave the country at all, not be gone for four years missing a wife and little child. And I wouldn't come back with maybe a foot blown off, or shrapnel in my head, and just a few bucks in my pocket, my Army pay. I'd have a fortune in the bank, untaxed. Hell, I already had half a fortune, courtesy of Mr. Smith, and I hadn't done a damn thing yet. And to top it off, I'd gotten a college education and had no job at a time when everybody had jobs and my curve ball was nonexistent and I was never going to pitch in the major leagues anyway.

I found myself getting mad. I got angry with Smith for finding me in the first place, and dumping this horrific burden on me. But then again, someone had dumped that burden on him. That wasn't his fault, was it? The more I mulled it over, the madder I got. I even got mad at Kendrick, my classmate, who'd told that bullshit story to the reporter about me being an NRA champion, the story that got me into this goddamn mess. But mostly I got mad at the Kennedys.

Who the hell were these assholes to play God and put at risk, at needless risk, everything and everyone I ever cared about? Who were they to put me in this terrible position? What gave them the right? I pictured JFK on his yacht, the *Honey Fitz*, cruising along off Palm Beach or Cape Cod or someplace, on a beautiful day with his beautiful wife thinking beautiful thoughts, including how to play hide-the-missiles and yank Khrushchev's chain, ice Fidel with some exotic James Bond scheme and grab a few votes, all in time to dress in white tie for a five course meal and some ballroom dancing. That was fine for him; that's where he lived. But the rest of us dwelled in the sea he cruised over, in murky water swimming against the Gulf Stream with sharks and barracuda and moray eels snapping at us, all the while afraid his propeller would chew us up as we struggled to the surface for breath.

My dad, my uncles, they'd protected me. Without complaint, without hesitation. Didn't I have the job of protecting them, if I could? Ramon had given up everything, apparently without hesitation, and asked me to take care of his sister. I hadn't succeeded.

Suddenly, incredibly, I could have a direct role in finding my best friend and his dad, if they were alive somewhere, probably rotting in a Cuban prison. If relations eased with a new administration, one not hell-bent on killing another country's leader, Smith might actually be able to get them out. I might be able to find Mirasol. Maybe. It was a staggering concept. And if Smith got the job done with someone else – I had little doubt he would – I would have foregone my chances to help Ramon, Abelardo, Ramira, Mirasol. My backing out would have all been for nothing.

Two days later, the phone rang.

"Abelardo Figueroa was executed in the summer of 1961 at the prison at El Morro Castle along with over a hundred other insurgents. There is no word on Ramon Figueroa, but he's not on a death list. If he's in prison, it's most likely for thirty years. That's what most of them got."

My roommate, my teammate was languishing in jail. His blazing fastball and sweeping curve were never going to grace the major leagues. His father was dead. Those irresponsible bastards in the White House had shattered their family: made my best friend's mother a widow and broken the heart of his sister. I knew Ramon would risk his life to try and rescue me, if things were reversed. Hell, he *had* risked his life.

And there was one other thing. A thought I'd pushed down into my subconscious, a belief I couldn't deny. I knew something in my gut that couldn't be rationalized or reasoned away. It was overriding.

It was immaterial what I deduced, what my logic was, how I thought about the problem. It didn't matter if my anger was real, my reasoning sound, or anything. It was all chaff before the wind. What I deep down knew was a certainty. When I dared think about it, I felt sick to my stomach.

No matter what Smith said, no matter how beguiling his smile, persuasive his words, I knew too much. I knew way too much.

I was boxed in.

If I backed out, they would kill me.

All right. Okay. There it was. Once I faced that conclusion, once I realized I really had no choice, I grew calm, resolute. In my mind, I cleared the decks.

The time for choices had passed.

Chapter 17

I met the man the world would know as Lee Harvey Oswald in the second week of November, 1963. We met in a dingy Dallas bar, a nondescript place whose name may have been the Fun House. Actually, I wasn't supposed to meet him at all. We had been in Dallas since the first week of that month; Smith said it was important for me to get familiar with the layout of the city and its routes of transportation. He also had, apparently, other things to do in Dallas because he was constantly busy. As was our modus operandi, we stayed in two different hotels. Once again, Smith registered at an upscale place called the Adolphus, while I checked into the White Plaza, maybe ten or fifteen minutes walking distance away. Nice enough, but probably built before Texas statehood. Smith had brought his Impala: I wondered if he drove it around the country or had it sent. Maybe he had a driver.

He had said the president was going to be in Texas before the end of November, and Dallas would be the scene of a parade. Kennedy wanted exposure and this looked like the best opportunity to make our move. After a few drinks in a Dallas hotel bar, Smith let drop the news that we were actually in town a couple of days before the Secret Service even knew the trip was still on, following demonstrations against Stevenson in Dallas October 24. He said he had been aware of the Texas commitment since June, although no dates had been set then. I seemed to learn the most when Smith got a few under his belt. It didn't happen often, though.

"What aren't you aware of?" I asked. Smith just smiled. After another cocktail, we went to a restaurant Smith liked - he seemed to know where to eat in every town - called the Cattlemen's Steak House, or something similar.

"We have a second marksman for the team," he announced, over his prime rib. Team? Smith had originally talked about the possibilities of a second shooter, and even triangulated fire, but this was the first I knew we would have another gunman. "For you, this is going to make things a lot easier."

As yet no one knew the route Kennedy's parade was going to take, maybe not even Smith. Therefore it was not possible to work out any positioning or placement.

I swallowed a bite of steak. The portions were big enough for two people. Smith was right, the food was delicious. It had a savory flavor, like juicy smoke. If you couldn't get good steak in Texas, where could you?

"Who is this guy?" I asked. I was very curious to find out if he was a professional or military operative. Maybe he was just another target shooter who happened to drop in on the local hammer-and-sickle barbecue, like me.

"You're never going to meet him," Smith said, "and he won't have to meet you. I'll coordinate between the both of you. You'll each have input as to how this thing will be set up, once we pick the site. That way, neither of you can compromise the other. Much safer."

"What? How is that going to work? Of course I have to meet him," I said.

112

"No you don't. You have to understand," explained Mr. Smith. "Everything is on a need-to-know basis. Compartmentalized. That's how we work. It's a matter of security. This is elementary. I have to work like that too."

"I don't care about that," I said, putting down my fork. "I damn sure am going to meet this guy if we're going to go much further." This was really upsetting me. Now I was upsetting Smith.

"That's impossible. You have to understand this," said Smith. He was getting frustrated. "Everything will still be coordinated just fine. You'll just communicate through me."

I dug in my heels. "No way. I don't give a shit about your rules. What we're doing is so incredibly risky I'm not going to put myself on the line with some guy I never even met who could get me killed or something and I'm not allowed to meet him. Screw your rules." I was really upset. I think a lot of suppressed emotions, apprehension, fear, and other baggage were suddenly pouring out, and this issue was the catalyst. There was a lot more stress than I realized.

Smith eyed me for a time. He must have realized it, too. "All right. Maybe it's best anyway, but I really don't think so. I don't want you getting all worked up on me. I'll arrange for you to meet him in the next day or so." He motioned for me to eat.

"Don't let it spoil your dinner," he said, dryly. It certainly wasn't going to spoil his.

*　　*　　*　　*　　*　　*

So here we were in this Texas rub joint spending one of the most irritating hours of my life. It didn't take long to realize maybe Mr. Smith might have had a good idea for us never to meet. Right away I could see Al Hidell – as Smith introduced him - was going to be a problem. Maybe 5'9", his difficult nature was evident from our introduction.

"Call me Ozzy," he said. It was downhill from there.

"Are you a Marxist?" he asked straightaway.

"I loved *Animal Crackers*." I do have a sense of humor.

"What is that, a joke?" he demanded.

No, it's a movie, I thought, but didn't say it.

"Well, I'm not going to get into philosophical discussions," I answered, instead.

"Why not?" This was, apparently, typical Ozzy Hidell belligerent dialogue. Strident little bastard. He seemed to spit out his words.

"Let's just be professionals about this, all right?" I responded. Hidell just glared at me. This kept him quiet for a time, but he soon went at it again. I hoped Mr. Smith would help me with this, but he didn't. I guess he figured I had asked for it. And I was being well-paid.

We were on our second beers when Smith went to make a phone call. While he was gone, Hidell told me he had been to Mexico, where he had worked with government officials involving some cloak-and-dagger scheme, and hinted that he had carried out a government-sanctioned assassination operation a few months prior. My skepticism was apparent. Hidell said the target was an American general. I did not recall reading about any general being killed, but I suppose I could have missed it. I could not believe Mr. Smith would recruit someone like this, but his money was real enough. Maybe the two of them went around killing everybody.

The Man on the Grassy Knoll

And later, on our third beers, when Smith went to the rest room:

"Don't you believe the CIA breaks the law for their own ends?" he pestered. I already knew the answer to that, didn't I? Didn't he? What had Smith told him? Or maybe, what had Smith told me?

"Do you believe this guy Smith?" He nodded his head toward the rest room door. "Do you believe he is who he says he is? You don't think his name is really Smith, do you? Do you really think he works for who he says?"

Now these were interesting questions. Of course, I had wondered myself from the beginning. I wanted to know what Ozzy had to say.

"Who does he say he works for?" I asked. Ozzy didn't answer me, but looked at me in that pissed-off little pursed lips way of his.

I prodded again. "Well, he has the credentials, doesn't he?"

"What the hell, are you kidding me?" Ozzy was getting excited again. Evidently this was his normal state. Sometimes little guys are like that. "Would you know the real thing from what he showed you? You made him show you I.D., didn't you? Did you try and check up on this guy?"

"How the hell would I do that?" I asked. I could be belligerent too.

He didn't answer. He had a brooding look, and there was something funny about his eyes. I imagined he saw all right, since he was supposed to be a marksman, but it was as though the light was unnaturally bright and if you looked closely it was cracked. I did not want to look too closely, anyway. I began to get nervous. The less Mr. Hidell knew

115

about me, the better. Smith was right. I could certainly see why he didn't want me to meet this psycho. If anyone was going to get caught, it would likely be one of us, not Smith, who would not have a rifle to worry about. If Ozzy were nabbed, I certainly did not want him to know anything about me.

Hidell bragged on about his marksmanship and his military background.   He told me he was a Marine sharpshooter and again hinted at involvement in other 'missions.' I did not think this was likely true, but then again here he was in Dallas. Until meeting Hidell, Smith had not mentioned the possibility of another participant since June or July. I speculated that Ozzy was a last minute player, but it was possible I was kept uninformed until right before the event - Mr. Smith's need-to-know philosophy. I wondered what weapon he would be using. Did he also have the Tokarev? I asked him about it.

"It's an Italian sniper rifle," he said.

"What kind?"

"You'll see."

I tried one more time to make conversation.

"Did Mr. Smith get it for you?"

He looked at me, incredulous. "What are you, crazy?" I wanted to pop him. I might have if Smith hadn't returned to the table.

On Friday, a week before the motorcade, the Times-Herald printed a story saying the Trade Mart was a likely site for the Presidential luncheon that was planned in Dallas. I had hoped to see the Peter, Paul and Mary concert the following Saturday night, but Kennedy would arrive a day earlier. Mr. Smith brought over another Dallas city map - he had marked up one or two already - and began tracing possible motorcade routes. Doubtless the Republic National Bank of Dallas would pale if it knew to what purpose their complimentary maps were being used.

It was just the two of us, and I imagined it was because Ozzy was at work. It appeared the number of routes to the Trade Mart would be very limited, if the luncheon was really going to be held there. Mr. Smith pointed out only a few variations: there were actually two streets running parallel for a time - Main and Elm. Smith felt the motorcade would likely take Main Street because that's where the crowd would be, especially from the office windows that lined that avenue. There was another variation near the airport - I do not recall what streets were involved. Smith remarked that the likely route would take the entourage right past Al Hidell's place of employment - an extraordinary stroke of luck, if that was going to be the case. That is when I learned Ozzy worked in the School Book Depository, an apparent irony that would help shape the history of the last half of the 20th century. If Hidell was being paid the same amount I was, or anywhere close, then I assumed he was only working for ready access to the School Book Depository windows. Smith was confident the motorcade was going to go right past Ozzy's building, although to my knowledge this information was not published until the following Tuesday in the Times-Herald.

Smith said the set-up was perfect, if Hidell could conceal himself by a window overlooking the parade route. Mr. Smith said he was not familiar with the building from the inside, nor what floor Ozzy worked on, and so he was anxious to talk to him. He knew, though, that the building was tall, perhaps seven or eight stories, with what appeared to be a clean view of the motorcade's planned route of travel. As we studied the map, noting the hairpin turn onto Elm from Houston, we realized the motorcade would have to be traveling at a crawl. We had not yet reconnoitered the second point of fire, but it appeared the rail yard area down the street from Ozzy's warehouse might work.

Later in the day, Mr. Smith picked me up and we drove out to the site, which was just a couple of blocks from his hotel anyway. We studied the layout. The entire area, known as Dealey Plaza, formed somewhat of a semi-enclosed theater. It was apparent that the two points of fire would be a window from the warehouse and somewhere along the rail yard area, on the north side of Elm Street. It looked like Ozzy would actually have a better shot as the motorcade approached the hairpin turn, rather than after, but in that case our fire would not be coordinated. Also, there was no way to ensure the motorcade would then follow the preplanned route toward me. Even if it did, the limousine would likely be speeding by the time it neared my location.

From Elm, a hill sloped upward to the yard, on the north side, just before a railroad overpass. This bridge, of course, would have been ideal, but there was no cover and certainly that area would be patrolled or cleared. The rail yard, on the other hand, seemed attractive. There was a wooden picket fence, maybe 5' high, with trees and shrubs here and there. The fence was between a pavilion, toward the warehouse, and the overpass. We parked about a block away and walked up to the fence from the yard side. The place seemed deserted, although there were cars in the parking lot behind us. We noted a low watchtower by the tracks, actually just a two story building, but saw no movement near it. A

118

small stand of trees grew near a place where the fence angled back, and this looked to provide concealment. The fence was a bit low; I had hoped it would be possible to use it as a rifle rest, with a minimal barrel length protruding from the pickets. Examining the fence, though, the pickets were at a steep angle and close together. The only angle would be straight ahead, which was unworkable. The barrel couldn't rest on top, either, because the pickets were so pointed. I would have to abandon that idea. We stayed there about thirty or forty minutes. During that time, there was no foot traffic within 100 yards. There were really no other choices, and these sites looked realistically workable. As the motorcade would approach me, I was within 25 or 30 degrees of being in a direct line, and the target would be moderately traversing my field of fire. If the target came closer, the angle increased sharply until it would pass by at about 90 degrees. I worked all this out as I studied the layout.

Depending on where I stood, the view up Elm Street was partially obscured by the trees, unless I abandoned their cover, and to some extent the pavilion retaining wall. I walked toward the overpass until I found the best accommodation between concealment and a clear field of fire. Allowing for the distance required for the motorcade to clear the trees and the retaining wall, giving me an unobstructed target, I pictured the location of the limousine at the optimum point. The distance was quite close. Using a 3' stride - I was pretty accurate from years of pacing off targets - I measured off the distance from the picket fence to the curb and added another ten to twelve feet to the target. It came out to be exactly one hundred feet. Estimating back to a farther point for a minimal angle, depending on where I stood behind the fence, the maximum distance appeared to be between 150 and 175 feet.

One hundred feet. Was I really going to be within one hundred feet of the President of the United States, aiming a Soviet sniper rifle? How could I miss? I didn't have to be a marksman for this job. I could hit him with my fast ball. I had worried about having enough magnification, but at this distance the 4X scope would be plenty, especially with a moving target and uncertain rifle rest.

It was also evident that Ozzy Hidell would be firing first, perhaps by several seconds. That meant I might not be firing at all, should he be successful, or something unpredictable happen. I hoped that would be the case. If Hidell really was a crack shot, it should be the case. But I wasn't up for giving any refunds.

The one thing that could hurt us now was the weather. Inclement weather meant no open convertible. Mr. Smith explained that Kennedy would then use the 'bubbletop', which was weather-resistant but not bulletproof. That meant the first shot might be unreliable; it could glance off or go straight through or do just about anything. Hopefully it would still hit the target but if not, chances are it would take out the bubble for the second round. I brought up the logic for hollow point vs. the copper jacketed cartridge for Ozzy's Italian rifle, since he would be shooting at the bubble first. Smith said Hidell was not able or not going to use any special ammunition. He just dismissed the subject. I assumed at the time it was because Ozzy was just too far away to rely on the less accurate hollow point cartridge.

In any event, Mr. Smith was monitoring the weather forecasts closely.

The Man on the Grassy Knoll

We spent perhaps ten minutes looking over possible escape routes. I was uncomfortable with my rearward exposure. Things were too wide open. I asked Mr. Smith to provide a cover vehicle, maybe a panel truck, parked behind me, near the point where the fence angled back. He pointed out that any vehicle near the scene might be scrutinized, but he would consider it. I was also being provided with phony Secret Service credentials, in case I needed to flash some I.D. while getting the hell out of there. I took some comfort in the lengths they were going to protect me. Of course, they were really protecting themselves. If I got away, they got away. If I got caught, the credentials were phony anyway so there would be no real link to Smith's outfit or any other government agency. Partially for the same reason, I was going to have to walk the fifteen or twenty minutes - eight blocks or so - back to my hotel. This was an uncomfortable thought, though Smith tried to assure me there was no real reason to be anxious about the idea.

Since I was a non-smoker, Smith was going to bring a number of cigarette butts to scatter around what became known as Site Y among us. Ozzy Hidell, of course, was Site X. Mr. Smith's code names. The purpose of the smokes was to leave a false clue. For the same reason, I had purchased a pair of common shoes one size too small, so that any footprints would not match my shoe size.

Strange as it may seem, that day, for the first time, I began to realize this thing could actually happen. It could be pulled off with no more talent and organization than I had seen, and that was not overwhelming with Ozzy Hidell in the group. As we got back into Smith's car, I was reminded of something.

"You said the Cuban operation had the code name Zapata, and that everything has a code name," I said.

"That's right," he replied.

"I've been meaning to ask you. Does this operation have a code name?"

"Sure it does," he said. "Kidron."

Kidron? What the hell was that?

I should have looked it up. I really should have.

Chapter 18

On Monday or Tuesday evening of the following week - I'm pretty sure it was Monday but my notes are unclear on the date - we met with Ozzy Hidell in a small taproom somewhere outside the downtown area. I had suffered through a mediocre barbecue at some place called Bell's with Mr. Smith - evidently he was determined to try every barbecue joint in the Dallas area, because he had a list. It was proving a bad idea, at least for me. The damn thing was alphabetic, starting with Austin's and ending with Underwood's, I think. Who would do that? I couldn't believe it. Smith never got a spot of sauce on any of his white shirts, but I would leave dripping the stuff, no matter how hard I tried. Also, I was getting sick of the same food; a little barbecue went a long way as far as I was concerned.

On the way over, Mr. Smith explained Ozzy had no car and so we were meeting near his home. We sat in another back booth. I sipped a beer and, Smith, uncharacteristically, was drinking coffee. Hidell was agitated, but did not elaborate. He referred more than once to "that bitch." Evidently he was having woman trouble. He wasn't the only excited person in that bar; the guys two booths over were arguing loudly about the upcoming SMU game. I thought some Baylor fan was going to get poked. I was sure Hidell had picked this dive to meet - what a no-class guy. Mr. Smith

123

ignored this distraction and Ozzy's obvious anger while he reviewed our situation:

1. Fortuitously, the motorcade was to run right past Ozzy Hidell's job. He would not have to travel to another site and might be able to pre-position his weapon. His presence in the warehouse would not be questioned.

2. The hairpin turn by the warehouse assured a reasonably slow speed for the target.

3. The confined space allowed less maneuverability for the motorcade.

4. Considering the target and its level of protection, the distances were quite close.

5. Ozzy Hidell's straight line trajectory and elevation were very favorable.

6. Listening to the sounds of car horns, etc., while we were on the scene, we observed that sound reverberated throughout the area. This would help create confusion as to the source of the gunfire.

Without a suppressor on the Tokarev, this was of key importance.

For my part, the route would work well. The picket fence in front of the rail yard and the trees provided concealment, though the limousine might not always be completely visible around the turn area. By the time the motorcade got to me Site Y should provide a clear, close target, although the speed was questionable. The escape route, however, was still disquieting. There was a real possibility of encountering any number of people, and disposal of the rifle needed to be addressed. I knew I might have to rely on the subterfuge of the phony Secret Service credentials. Mr. Smith said he had a few ideas and would solve the problem.

The Man on the Grassy Knoll

Finally, Smith revisited the bubbletop question, should it rain. Rain caused me a few problems, too, in my exposed position. It was entirely possible Hidell's first shot, coming before mine, would take out the bubbletop and I had to be prepared to fire rapidly if the limousine sped up. I asked if the bubbletop might craze after being hit, so that it would be impossible to see inside. No one had any idea.

Hidell, after another drink, tried to drift the conversation to his woman problems. I didn't need to hear it, and tried to tune him out.

I really did not like speaking with the man; he was so difficult. Everything was bad, everybody was against Ozzy Hidell, and he was going to make the system pay. I had avoided all philosophical discussions about politics, government, or anything else, really, but it did not matter. You heard an entire conversation from Hidell whether you were a part of it or not. Smith seemed to have a great deal of patience with this nut case. I didn't really get it.

Realizing he was getting no sympathy for his difficulties, Hidell brought up the problem of his rifle. He apparently was driven to work every day by a co-worker who lived nearby. Ozzy needed to get the weapon from his garage to the warehouse. He said he would break the gun down first, which only took a couple of minutes, but still didn't want to have to explain a roughly three foot long package to his driver. Could we keep it for him or allow him to retrieve it and take it downtown?

I looked at Mr. Smith. He was thinking about this transportation issue.

"You mean now?" I asked.

"Well, sometime before Friday, then," Ozzy said. "But getting it out of there might be a little tricky."

I didn't know what he meant. For some reason Mr. Smith didn't like this. He still hadn't said anything. Finally, he expressed his thoughts. "I don't want all three of us in the same car if we have to retrieve your rifle. I don't ever want all three of us in the same car at any time."

"Want me to take him?" I asked.

"Not really," was the reply.

Hidell spoke up. "John can do it. It'll be all right. I'll just get the gun and we can put it in the trunk or whatever we want to do with it until Friday. But I've got to break it down first so I can take it inside."

He meant at the warehouse. Evidently he didn't have access at night or didn't want to risk leaving it unattended overnight.

"Graves can just wait up the street. It'll be just a couple of minutes."

Mr. Smith, from his expression, was not too pleased but I suppose there was not going to be a great many choices.

"I think I should go instead of John," he said, finally.

"No, dammit," said Ozzy. "Besides, I want John to see my rifle. He can drive me. What is the problem, anyway?"

"I can do it, Mr. Smith. This is not going to break my brain." I was hoping some time alone with Ozzy Hidell might yield some illuminating answers to certain questions. Particularly about Mr. Smith.

So it was agreed I would drive Mr. Smith's Impala the next night, with Ozzy, so he could transport his Italian rifle without his commuting driver having to see a suspicious package. Ozzy gave me directions to his house, which was nearby, and things seemed workable enough. The address was 1026 North Beckley. I was to park at the corner and he would join me about eight o'clock.

After supper the next evening, I made my way to Mr. Smith's hotel and telephoned him from the lobby. While I waited for him to come down, I admired the fine furnishings and antiques I was sure were genuine. There were no antiques in my lobby, unless you counted the whole hotel. In a few minutes, Mr. Smith appeared and handed me the keys to the Impala. As usual, he cautioned me to obey all traffic laws and avoid any incident, especially with Ozzy Hidell in the car. By now, I was used to this. He walked me out to the Impala.

"I really don't think -," he began.

"Please, Mr. Smith," I said. "You wanted me to become familiar with the Dallas layout, anyway. Everything will be okay."

My plan was to drive out of view and pull in the nearest place I could find. I would open the glove box and find out who the vehicle was registered to, and the address. This would probably be the only chance I would have to snoop on Mr. Smith.

"The registration is in the glove box," he said. "The name on the registration is Thomas Parrish. Don't let it throw you if you get stopped, which I am certain you won't because you are obeying every traffic sign, but just in case, that's me."

"This Parrish guy is you also?" I asked.

"Yes." So much for the glove box search.

I drove off in the direction of Hidell's house, but after a few blocks wheeled into a store parking lot anyway. Quickly, I opened the glove box and rummaged through it for any useful material. Sure enough, the registration was to a Thomas Parrish of Falls Church, Virginia. Nothing else - no owner's manual, street maps, or even a Kleenex. I turned off the ignition and ran around to the trunk, which I opened. Maybe something was in there. Smith had gotten our secrecy agreement out of this same trunk, back in May - it seemed like half a lifetime ago. Maybe that was his mobile office. It was a long shot, but I had the chance, and I wasn't going to get it again.

Paydirt. Shoved back against the rear wall of the trunk was a cardboard file holder, held closed with a large rubber band. I carefully noted the position before retrieving it, although it certainly seemed it would slide around just from driving. I grabbed the folder, closed the trunk, and sat back down in the driver's seat. I turned on the light.

Inside the holder were two manila files. One contained a sheaf of papers, and the file tab was blank. The other was empty, but had a header on the tab. The header was typed **Task Force W - DFG.** I opened the file containing about ten pages.

Smith was, apparently, editing what appeared to be a manual. Or rather, loose leaf pages of a manual. Each page was double spaced and had the word DRAFT on top, probably where the heading would normally be. There were numbered sections and Smith seemed to have only certain parts. I looked at my watch. I was going to have to hurry to meet Hidell on the designated corner.

The overall theme seemed to be pointers on how to evade detection as an operative by avoiding common mistakes that would tip off a suspicious (unnamed) enemy. The object, apparently, was to blend in as an American businessman. It

128

was fascinating stuff. I skimmed as much as I could as fast as I could. One section described clothing and said that short sleeved white shirts were the mark of middle management, or lower, and that raincoat colors were a tip-off as to where the executive was on the corporate ladder. I didn't know any of this. Tan raincoats meant one thing; black raincoats another. I cannot recall which was higher management. I wondered if this stuff was true: if so, I had been right to liken corporate life to the military.

Another section noted that always asking for meal receipts, etc., was a sure sign of working for the government. Using pen and paper to figure out an exact gratuity - another civil service tip-off. Choice of restaurant for meeting purposes was discussed. Fascinating stuff, but it seemed kind of childish to me. I wondered if this all could really be valid.

Smith, or someone, had made corrections in pen to almost all the pages in the file. There was more, but everything was in the same general vein. It was actually kind of amusing. I shoved everything back into the folder, put it back in the trunk, and exited the parking lot. I had to hurry now.

On the way, I thought about what I had seen. Did this prove Smith CIA? My assumption when skimming the material had been this manual was going to be intended as a guide for U.S. intelligence field agents. But maybe it was to enhance detection, rather than avoid it. Maybe it was being written for foreign operatives, giving clues for spotting American intelligence personnel, or for masquerading as businessmen. It could be read either way, now that I thought about it.

The Man on the Grassy Knoll

Maybe Smith wasn't really editing the manual. Maybe the handwritten commentary was just notes intended for a reader, not the author. Maybe that wasn't really Smith's writing at all, and he'd obtained the material from clandestine sources. I didn't have any handwriting samples. Was he editing a manual for someone else, to tip his operatives off as to normal CIA or normal American businessman behavior? On balance, I thought the most likely conclusion to be that this was genuine CIA stuff, but who knew for certain?

I had no idea what the label **Task Force W - DFG** meant. Smith had never mentioned the name, of course, and there was no way I could find out short of asking him. I was certainly not about to do that. W... Washington? Weapon? Wing? Water? DFG... DeFense? DraFtinG? DeFoliatinG? Deep FreezinG? I kept this up until I got to Hidell's street.

I made it to the corner on North Beckley with two or three minutes to spare. The large house seemed well-kept, framed by attractive trellises and a neatly trimmed hedge. Ozzy was nowhere in sight. Rather than wait and possibly attract attention, I drove around for a block or two. When I returned, Hidell was coming down the street, empty-handed.

"Where's the rifle?" I asked. Ozzy seemed surprised.

"What do you mean? We have to go get it."

"I thought you said it's in your garage," I said.

"Yeah, it is, but that's not here. This is just a rooming house. My house is out in Irving."

"What?"

"My house is out in Irving," he repeated. "I just stay here during the week because it's much closer to work."

No wonder the house seemed large.

"Well, where the hell is Irving?"

130

The Man on the Grassy Knoll

"Just follow my directions," he said.

Irving turned out to be a long way from where I picked up Ozzy Hidell. I could see why he had a place close to downtown. We approached the street Ozzy said he lived on. He had me drive very slowly.

"Okay," he said. "That's it, there." He pointed to his house. Lights were on inside.

"Who's staying at your house?" I asked. "The lights are on."

"Just don't worry about it," he said. "Let me out here. The rifle's in the garage. I'll break it down and bring it out in this bag."

I was maybe half a block away. Hidell approached the house like he didn't want to be seen. I couldn't understand what was going on. If this was his house, why was he acting like he was going to break in? Then I couldn't see him anymore.

I waited for at least ten minutes. I was starting to freak out, imagining a thousand watt patrol car spotlight lighting me up at any moment while Ozzy committed some felony down the street. Suddenly, out of the darkness, here came Hidell, but instead of a cloth bag he had a blanket. He got in the passenger side, cursing and upset. He left the door ajar so the light stayed on.

"The goddamn thing is stuck," he said. He unraveled the blanket. "I can't get it. Got any coins?" He uncovered his pride and joy.

*   *   *   *   *   *

I was speechless. I could think of nothing to say. We had gone down the rabbit hole and the White Rabbit was looking at his timepiece because it was way too late.

131

The Man on the Grassy Knoll

The object of my stupefaction was this piece of shit toy rifle, this Mattel excuse for a gun, that Ozzy Hidell had uncovered.

"I got it mail order."

With what, Raleigh coupons? S&H Green Stamps? I couldn't tell if he was bragging or being defensive. I didn't even see a brand name on it. This supposed ex-Marine sharpshooter was going to exercise the one-man, one-vote principle with a copper-jacketed ballot from this piece of scrap iron? Was he going to throw it at Kennedy from the window?

Evidently Ozzy misinterpreted my open mouth for admiration. He said something complimentary about his rifle; I don't know what. Insanely, I was reminded of the old World War II joke my father told:

"Want to buy a thousand used Italian army rifles? Never fired. Dropped only once."

At that point in time I felt the stirrings of panic. Not only because of this lunatic, but because Smith had brought him into the picture. What kind of judgment was that? What kind of operation was this?

"How much did it cost?"

"What do you care?"

"I'm curious, okay?"

"Twelve bucks. Twelve bucks and seventy eight cents mail order," he said.

I realized he actually *was* bragging, for God's sake. I looked again, trying to assimilate what I was seeing. Maybe I'm overlooking something, I thought. But no, the crude construction and generous tolerances could not be glossed over. Hidell would be lucky if this popgun didn't blow up in his face. No silencer, no flash hider, no nothing.

The Man on the Grassy Knoll

Even the grammar was wrong. It said, "MADE ITALY", conveniently omitting the preposition. Maybe they omitted something else small, like the trigger. I read the legend CAL 6.5 and a serial number, C2766. Pride of manufacture, as I said, was demonstrated by the absence of the manufacturer's name on this Italian - what - gondola oar? The sling looked like it came from Hidell's camera, or maybe a Daisy Red Ryder. Ozzy probably had about as much chance of hitting his target as he had of hitting the railroad overpass. Even the scope, as I recall, was a joke. A cheap four power Jap job, jerry-rigged with a side mount. Apparently the rifle wasn't even built to take a conventionally mounted scope. The manufacturer must not have dreamed anyone would want one.

Maybe it was a magic wand, I thought. Hidell was going to wave it at the president and he'd just fall over. My mind does things like that sometimes. Meanwhile, there we were, on an Irving street with the dome light on and a rifle in Mr. Smith's front seat.

"Give me a coin, for Chrissake," he said again. I reached in my pocket and pulled out a bunch of change. Ozzy grabbed a dime and tried to use it as a screwdriver.

"I've done this before," he said. "Now the goddamn thing's not coming apart." No, just me. I was coming apart.

"This isn't working, Ozzy. What do you want to do?" We couldn't just sit there all night working on his rifle. I could just see us explaining all this to the Irving Police Department, let alone Mr. Smith.

"JUST SHUT UP A GODDAMN MINUTE," he snapped, furious. Finally he stopped and threw the coin at the dashboard. It bounced back and hit the rifle barrel with a clink. I almost laughed.

133

The Man on the Grassy Knoll

"OK, shit," he said. "I'm gonna have to come back. I can work on it in the garage. The goddamn thing. It'll be OK. Shit. I didn't want to bring it in on my way to work. Now I've gotta come back out here again."

I sure as hell didn't want to come out here again, that much I knew. With a quick motion, Hidell wrapped the blanket around the recalcitrant gun. Before I could say anything, he jumped back out of the car and took off toward the house.

"Be right back," he hissed. I hoped he wouldn't.

He returned in just a minute. I was tired, aggravated, and a little scared at the Amateur Hour this was turning into. Just to make me feel better about the whole thing, Ozzy said, "Don't tell Smith. I'll take care of everything." Neither of us spoke much after that.

I drove him back to his rooming house, reflecting on the evening's bumbling events. I wondered if I still could back out and keep the money. Or maybe just back out.

But then something struck me. Was there a message here? Clearly, the "MADE ITALY" cheap rifle was not provided by Smith's armament supplier. Why not get him a real weapon? Was this another game within a game? A glimmer of possible understanding finally began to glow inside me.

The glow became incandescent. No wonder this loose cannon, this shrimpy psychopath, had been brought in. Ozzy Hidell, somehow, was going to be the safety valve. The possible patsy. The grand diversion. I had the weapon, I had the money, I would have the escape route. Ozzy would be firing first, and maybe that was no coincidence. His fire would be likely to draw immediate and perhaps overwhelming

134

response; his sniper nest would be the flashpoint for the law; his rifle barrel sticking out a window, with no cover, silencer or flash hider would be the focus of every Dallas city cop, every Secret Service agent, every U.S. Marshall, every Texas Ranger, every Sheriff's deputy. The motorcade would continue away from Ozzy Hidell and right into my field of fire with everyone going the other way. Given the confusing acoustics of the area, no one might even know I was shooting. He would never have time to get out of that building before it was swarming with lawmen. No wonder Hidell was still on the job; the parade route may have indeed been an incredible coincidence but now I was beginning to doubt it.

There was something I needed to know. We were nearing his rooming house.

"Ozzy," I said. "When did you start working in the book warehouse?"

"Oh, mid-October."

"How'd you get the job?" I asked.

"What are you, a cop?" No. I wasn't a cop. But enough of a sleuth to realize this was four months after Mr. Smith said he knew John Kennedy was coming to Dallas. He may not have known the details back in June, but he knew the President was coming.

I dropped Hidell off and got the hell out of there. He never even said thanks. I was almost falling asleep at the wheel, but some part of my brain was still churning, along with my stomach. I could understand now why Smith hadn't wanted me to meet Ozzy Hidell. More to the point, he hadn't wanted Hidell to meet me. It looked like we might be headed in two different directions, and only mine was out of town. Mr. Smith might never tell me directly, but perhaps I was

135

gaining an understanding. Very possibly Smith was playing an involved chess game while we were pecking away at Chinese checkers. In some crazy way, I gained more confidence in the entire operation although I fully realized I was, more than ever, looking through a glass darkly.

Chapter 19

Time was now a real factor and we still had not satisfactorily addressed the issue of my exit. On Thursday morning, Smith picked me up and we went to breakfast; I believe it was a Waffle Shop. Smith ordered a western omelet, I think, and just shook his head when I asked for corned beef hash with eggs.

"The joys of youth," he said. "If I ate like you, I'd have to work out the rest of the day to keep the weight off." Actually, it looked like he worked out a good part of the day. He turned to the business at hand.

"I think we've solved the problem with the rifle and the additional cover you wanted from the rail yard," he said.

"I'm all ears," I said.

"I don't think you've been very comfortable about wearing gloves." How the hell did he know that? Mrs. Dell?

"This might solve that aspect, also. We've prepared a drop-off vehicle."

"What's that?" I asked.

"It's in the parking lot." He meant by his hotel, not mine, as his was set in a more secure area. "We'll take a look at it in after we finish eating. We'll park this car right behind Site Y tomorrow morning, as close as we can get. We've rigged a false floor in the back. All you have to do is reach in the rear window, which will be down, or open the door. Pull

137

up the panel and lay the rifle down. There's a tab I'll show you. Then drop the panel and the gun is gone. After you use it, we'll get the car out of there."

I was impressed. It seemed Mr. Smith had improvised quickly and come up with a good solution. The Russian rifle was now probably an unnecessary touch, but maybe I'd have to drop it right at the fence. Or worse. I didn't want to think about that possibility.

"We need to talk about Ozzy Hidell," I said.

"No, we don't," said Mr. Smith. "I understand your concerns and you don't need to voice them. It's not something for you to worry about."

"I wouldn't agree."

"You'll have to trust me on this."

I was pretty sure now my assessment of the Ozzy Hidell situation was correct, or else that crackpot held some trump card of which I was unaware.

Our food came. I mixed the eggs and a few drops of hot sauce into the hash. They were done just right and it all tasted delicious. We ate for awhile. I polished off the hash and ate a piece of Texas toast.

I sipped my coffee. It was good and strong. It was time to bring up a difficult subject.

"Mr. Smith," I said, "I'm glad you brought up the subject of trust a little while ago. I have to trust you with my life, really. And I have to trust that the rest of the money will wind up in my bank account."

Mr. Smith looked at me with his half-smile.

"I need you to know, though, that I thought I needed some insurance."

The Man on the Grassy Knoll

That got his attention right away. The half-smile disappeared. I didn't tell Mr. Smith I also wanted some insurance in case they had some plans for me more drastic than just stiffing me on the money.

I continued. "You've known pretty much all about me even before we met. I know next to nothing about you, but a couple of things I do know make me a little cautious."

They made me a lot cautious. I paused, but he didn't ask what they were. So I told him.

"You got me involved thinking Fidel Castro was the target because you knew you couldn't get somebody cold turkey to go after the real target. A lot of guys, probably, would think going after Castro was defending the country. So you manipulated me.

'Secondly, I think I have a good idea how Ozzy Hidell fits in here. I don't like Hidell, in fact the little shit probably deserves whatever happens to him. But be that as it may. I need to know you'll honor the agreement we made and help me with the rest of the plan to get away after the mission.

'So I took a little insurance. Frankly, you're not going to like it much and I'm sorry. But we're playing in the biggest game maybe in the history of the United States, certainly in the history of me, and I can't afford to take any chances."

Mr. Smith was still as a statue. I don't even think he blinked since I started. His eggs were going to get cold. I paused and sipped my coffee, mostly for dramatic effect.

"Mr. Smith, I've got a couple of nifty souvenirs from our hotel meals. A juice glass and a dinner glass. Your juice glass and your dinner glass. They've got your fingerprints all over them. Now I'm pretty sure your fingerprints are on file somewhere. If you really work for the intelligence

139

community, they're no doubt on some government card there. If not, they probably are on file somewhere else. My tableware is in a really safe place, like a safety deposit box, with instructions I know I don't need to go into. The contents of that box are perfectly safe and won't be revealed provided you fulfill your part of the bargain. Please don't take this personally."

Mr. Smith stayed stock-still. His coffee had stopped steaming. The wheels were turning furiously, I knew. He must have evaluated all his options. Now we were chained together. If one jumped overboard, the other drowned.

His sardonic half-smile returned. "I won't take it personally. Maybe you've got a long term future with us."

Chapter 20

We finished breakfast and went outside to Smith's car. He drove to his hotel; Smith chatted as though our last conversation had not even taken place. I was relieved. My bravado had been as much acting as real. He was very professional about the whole thing. Either that or he was going to shoot me in the parking lot. We entered the lot and Smith drove toward the back of the area. He stopped in front of, evidently, the drop-off car. We got out. There was no one around. Things like no one being around seemed to work for Mr. Smith, I had noticed.

"OK," he said, unlocking the vehicle. He lifted the buttons on both back doors and wound the windows down. "Look inside here." He motioned for me to stick my head inside the opposite window. We both peered in. There was a false floor, higher than the real floor, and there was no drive train hump. The carpet seemed to match all right, but overall it didn't look too real.

"It doesn't look too real," I said.

He looked pained. "Please, John. Now look where I'm pointing. See the tab?" There was a tab next to the door. It stuck up maybe six inches. I put my hand on it. "There's one over here, too, in the exact same place." I saw the opposite tab. I could use the device from either side.

The Man on the Grassy Knoll

"Pull it up," he said. I lifted and the floor hinged up from the front seat. I had expected it to lift from the back. Then I saw they probably would have had no place to hinge the cover. The rifle would fit easily, even with the scope. I lowered the floor and saw how well the carpet blended together. I suppose I had not appreciated the workmanship, but it still looked false.

"It looks like it'll work really well," I said. "It'll have to be fast."

"It'll be as fast as you are. Maybe you want to practice walking up and leaning in and going through the motion. Also, you can open the door if that's easier or you want to keep the rifle low. But every second is going to count." He didn't need to tell me that.

So I pretended I was carrying the Tokarev and went through the motions a couple of times. After all, it wasn't that complicated. Once, though, I pulled the tab and it slipped out of my hand and the false bottom fell back down. That wouldn't be good.

Someone looking at us from a window would think we were a couple of nuts playing charades. I looked around. We were not in plain view of anyone.

"Why couldn't you just leave a car with an unlocked trunk? There are still plenty of cars around that open with a latch or a button and don't need a key." Not my Olds 98, though.

"Several reasons. First, it's more dangerous to open a car trunk because you are more likely to be seen. The trunk lid raises up in the air. Second, the only reason to open a trunk is to put something in or take something out. That means there's a greater chance of arousing suspicion, especially right after the intercept." That was one word I had never heard him use before. "Third, closing a trunk lid usually makes noise, unless you are very careful, and you are going to be in a hurry. And finally, we don't have an older car like that readily available, anyway."

"That's the first time I ever heard there was a limit to what you people can do," I said. "I didn't know you had any limitations."

"Our friend in Cuba would say we are nothing but limitations," Smith replied.

"It still bothers me that this dummy floor doesn't look real," I said. "It works fine and all, but anyone can see it's fake."

"John, sure they could see it if they were going to take a lot of time and scrutinize the car. But it's not going to be like crossing the border. There's going to be panic and yelling and everyone scrambling around and it only has to work for a few minutes until we get the car out of there. Besides, what are you worried about? You'll be long gone. It's the driver that'll have to worry, if anybody. And he's not going to be worried, believe me."

"Are you going to be the driver?" I asked.

Mr. Smith's sardonic grin returned. "No way."

                *   *   *   *   *

As we left the parking lot, I asked Smith if he wanted to go to the movies. I needed to do something to take my mind off the next couple of days. My choices for companionship were limited to two, and Ozzy Hidell certainly wasn't at the top of my guest list. I also wanted to make sure Mr. Smith really wasn't too upset with me for my little insurance plan.

Besides, he had the car.

"You want to go to the movies?" he asked. He looked surprised. "Entertainment isn't high on my list right now."

I persisted. "Come on, it'll take your mind off this whole thing."

"That's what I'm afraid of," he replied. He looked at me and slowly shook his head. "He wants to go to the movies," he said, to no one in particular.

I persisted. As I recall, we had the choice of some Jack Lemmon comedy or a John Wayne picture called McClintock, which was playing at the theatre right across the street from my hotel. Without a car my choices were down to one. I figured a guy like Smith would go for the western, but no sale. Maybe he was a little edgy, but there was no way to really tell. His display of hysteria would probably be raising an eyebrow. I could have used the distraction; my spring was wound pretty tightly. As it was, the rest of November 21 passed with an exasperating slowness. I tried to go to sleep early, but the night passed fitfully. I was sure Mr. Smith was sleeping like a baby, and God only knew what Ozzy Hidell dreamt about.

The Man on the Grassy Knoll

Chapter 21

Friday Nov 22 11:53 am

Smith drives slowly through the rail yard parking lot. We approach Site Y. As we draw near, we see the drop-off vehicle positioned near the fence, next to a station wagon that has been parked in an adjacent space. The wagon will provide additional cover, as I had initially requested, but it's not one of Smith's vehicles. We verify the windows of the drop-off car are down as planned. Mr. Smith stops his Impala; we get out and approach the fence. Smith is carrying a foul-smelling paper bag containing cigarette butts. Loosely covered with a blanket, I carry the Tokarev as unobtrusively as one can carry a sniper rifle with mounted scope, pointed down at the ground against my leg. Due to the proximity to target, I have opted for the hollow point cartridge. We stop about eight or ten feet west of the fence corner.

Smith dumps the cigarette butts over an area of several square feet. Wearing the shoes I had previously purchased one full size too small, I trample the butts into the ground. I lay the Tokarev down, and cover it with the blanket. From a distance, it might look like a picnic near the trees.

There is a huge car rental sign over the building where Ozzy Hidell, so far as we know, waits with his toy gun. Time and temperature light up digitally.

145

The Man on the Grassy Knoll

Hertz rents Chevrolets.

Is that where Smith got his car?

Both Smith and I are in jackets and ties. The earlier threat of rain has not materialized; it is breezy and clear. A beautiful day. The limousine will be open. The target is too close to be concerned about windage. Smith has the latest weather updates. He has been monitoring two cold fronts drifting around Texas, with thunderstorm activity; Dallas is supposed to be freezing by Sunday morning. Another reason to get the hell out of there. Weather-wise, we have hit it just right.

Smith looks around and indicates a group of people on the overpass. At least one is a police officer. I am finding it is one thing to know the area will be swarming with police; it is another to actually see them. I am hoping the officer will clear the overpass before the motorcade arrives.

"We've gone over everything about what you're to do afterward. Any last minute questions?" he asks.

"No. Believe me, I'm clear on that." Getting away is high on my list of priorities.

"Good luck, John." I am not prepared to be alone quite yet, but Smith, all business, turns and walks to his Impala. I will not see him again. Everything compartmentalized. I am completely alone, except for whatever bonds of fate tie me to that psychotic in the warehouse, half a block away, as we await our destiny.

My fear now is that other parade watchers, maybe even lawmen, will try to watch the motorcade from behind the fence.

There is time to kill. *Time to kill.* I pace the area, loll against the fence. The Tokarev lies under the blanket near me.

146

The Man on the Grassy Knoll

I could have used a coat, but the blanket will do double duty as I have solved the problem of the picket fence. There is still no one nearby. The crowd swells gradually as time for the motorcade's passing approaches. From my vantage point, I can see people lining the streets, leaning out office windows, leaning against guard rails from the overpass area. Still, Dealey Plaza is not overcrowded. I count about fifteen people on the overpass. Evidently it is not going to be cleared.

I am thinking about the station wagon. I have the cigarette butts, the shoes, and maybe I can create another red herring. There is a muddy area nearby; I don't know if it sprinkled here earlier but until mid-morning there were clouds and the potential for rain. Now the sky is clear and extremely bright. I deliberately step in the mud and walk to the station wagon, trying to leave a false trail of clear size eleven footprints to the wrong vehicle. I scrape the remaining mud off my shoes on the bumper of the wagon, so no other tracks will be present as I walk away. Anything I can do to throw off attention from the drop-off car may help.

I return to the fence area. I am still alone. It grows warmer; it must be around sixty. It has turned out to be a beautiful day. The colors seem larger than life, like a Technicolor movie. I wait. The longest half hour of my life.

Friday November 22 12:28 p.m.

In the distance, the noise of the approaching motorcade: the throaty roar of motorcycles and perhaps some cheers from the crowd. My heart begins to pound. I wipe my palms on my pants. I pat my pocket to make sure I have the phony Secret Service credentials. I still think I look way too young to be an agent. I really have to void my bladder.

147

The Man on the Grassy Knoll

Everybody out of the pool.

Squatting down, I pull back the blanket and again check the Tokarev. It is ready to fire. I wad the blanket up and wedge it between the pickets, letting the excess trail down the fence on my side. Now the weapon can pivot freely. I have my rifle rest. I wish it were maybe six or eight inches higher, but I don't want so much blanket that it could become an unsteady platform.

I look toward the warehouse but don't see anything.

Friday November 22 12:29 p.m.

The entourage is now visible. I can see it on Houston but it will be somewhat obstructed for several seconds when it snakes around the turn onto Elm. I make out a line of vehicles. Motorcycles precede the first car like flies around the beast. Smith said this will be a marked police car. There is supposed to be a space of several hundred yards, and then more cycles. The next vehicle is going to be an unmarked Dallas police car, and then the Presidential limousine. A whole bevy of vehicles follows the President's, but that is of no concern to me. Taking a deep breath, I bend down and pick up the Tokarev. I hold it just below the level of the fence; about five feet off the ground. The sounds of the Presidential motorcade increase. Glancing swiftly around, I determine that no one has moved any closer to my position and that all eyes are on the road. This includes all the police I can see.

Friday November 22 12:30 p.m.

The motorcade enters the hairpin turn. It is traveling quite slowly. My vision is obstructed for several seconds. Swiftly but unhurriedly, I raise the rifle and place the barrel

148

atop the blanket jammed into the picket fence. The weapon is now pointing toward Elm Street, toward the approaching vehicles. I allow several inches of the rifle to protrude to ensure the blanket won't catch fire, although I don't know if that is likely.

I look through the sight as the motorcade is now approaching. I pay no attention to the lead vehicles; I am looking only for the President's convertible limousine.

Cra-a-ck!!

Hidell has fired his first shot. I do not waver in my position.

A second or two later, much faster than I would have thought for a crude bolt action rifle:

Cra-a-ck!!

Hidell has squeezed off a second round. I take a deep draught of air and let half back out; I hold my breath.

Where the hell is the limousine?

Now I see it. It is on top of me; huge, looming in the scope. It has taken so long to arrive because, incredibly, unbelievably, the car has *slowed down.* The driver must be insane. He has virtually stopped and further exposed his passengers to a rain of deadly sniper fire, instead of speeding the hell out of there. Swiftly, I find President Kennedy. Somewhere in the back of my mind, there are two thoughts: one is the shock of seeing that familiar head all of us know so well from television and the newspapers. It indeed looms larger than real life, especially with four power magnification. The second flash is: *does the limousine driver work for Mr. Smith?*

John Kennedy is leaning forward and facing his left, toward his wife, exposing the entire right side of his head. I

The Man on the Grassy Knoll

have the suggestion of pink at the corner of my vision. I realize suddenly *he may be hit.* There is not enough time to be stunned. How the hell did Hidell actually hit him?

His arms are bent at the elbows and raised around his shoulders, as if blocking an unseen lineman. His expression is a combination of bewilderment and distress. I do not know where he has been wounded. I am steady and unwavering. The target is now almost stationary in my sight, quite close. The driver must still be on the brakes. Time and motion are standing still. Perhaps five or six seconds have elapsed since the second shot from the warehouse, an eternity in the Dallas sunlight. His right temple sits in my crosshairs. My view is crystal clear.

I cannot miss.

With even pressure, I squeeze the trigger on the Tokarev. Just at the moment of firing, I have the impression Ozzy may have fired again. The rifle kicks, but I do not lose the target in my scope. Quite clearly, I see the President's head explode and snap backward as a spray of blood and matter erupts to the rear. What is left of his head now jerks forward, a ghastly ruined thing. The hollow point has devastated the President; there is no doubt a second shot is not needed.

Now time accelerates madly. Drifting down the hill is a slight puff of smoke from the Tokarev, barely visible but tell-tale nonetheless. The thought flashes through my mind: I never told Smith about that problem, and now it might kill me. Beyond the puff, I see a motorcycle policeman swerve toward the curb and my position. In one motion I lower the gun, yank the blanket off the fence and drape it around the rifle - no time to wrap it.

The Man on the Grassy Knoll

I move swiftly around the station wagon and lean in the open back window of the drop-off car. Lifting the false floor, I place the rifle and blanket inside and drop the panel. This takes only a few seconds. I move away from the vehicle, but I am not running. Within moments, a cop, probably from the motorcycle, appears. Out of the corner of my eye, I see a half dozen or so people running from the overpass toward the parking lot.

Another uniformed officer has arrived; he wants to know who I am. My mind is in overdrive.

"Secret Service," I yell, flashing my 'credentials'. "Did you see anything?"

He responds, but I don't catch it. I look around and move off. A second person in civilian clothing challenges me; I repeat the performance. Now several police rush through the parking lot.

Swiveling my head, looking between cars, I drift away. Then I am gone.

Chapter 22

I walked briskly back to my hotel. Everywhere, in the streets, on the radio, news of the shooting was galvanizing Dallas. Entering the lobby, I took the elevator upstairs to my room and turned on the television. The story had flashed to almost every station. As far as I could tell, the press was announcing only that the President was wounded, perhaps gravely. I knew better. I was surprised by the inaccurate speculation and erroneous reporting but I had to get moving. As I watched, I stripped off my clothes. Everything went into a small duffel bag, including the size eleven shoes. There were no labels in the clothing or on the duffel. I zipped it closed and stepped into the shower. I scrubbed thoroughly to try and rid myself of any powder traces, dirt from the fence area, or any other microscopic links to Dealey Plaza. When I came out, Walter Cronkite was announcing the news that John F. Kennedy, 35th President of the United States of America, was dead. He almost broke down intoning the words.

I stopped, frozen. Somehow Walter Cronkite's pronouncement seemed more real to me than the actual event, as crazy as that sounds. I don't really know how to explain it. I'd grown up with Walter Cronkite; he brought the news to America. If he said it, it was true; you could bank on it. I felt faint, standing there with just a towel, and sat down heavily on the bed. I couldn't catch my breath. Then I ran into the bathroom and threw up violently. After splashing cold water on my face, I sat back down on the bed. I looked at my trembling legs. I felt cold and clammy, lightheaded; my stomach seemed as though the walls were touching.

I had to clear my mind for the tasks ahead. I bent over and put my head between my knees until I got my breath under control. It took several minutes to pull myself together.

My other suitcase was already packed and the change of clothes laid out on the bed. I dressed, checked around the room for any stray socks or other items, and picked up the suitcase and duffel bag. I left the room and went downstairs. There was a radio on and the clerk seemed in a fog. A few people were milling around the lobby, all talking about the shooting. Once checked out, I walked to the parking lot with my baggage. I found the car matching the description I was given and reached under the wheel well to the left rear tire as instructed. The keys were atop the tire. I placed the duffel containing the morning's clothing in the trunk. The other suitcase went in the car with me. Before I got in, though, I looked at the license plate. State of Texas. I committed the number to memory, and later wrote it (PJ 8611) on my airline ticket envelope, below the numbers from John Graves' passport (D092505) - and Social Security card (158 22 7577). This envelope later found its way into the safety deposit box along with the glassware, sidearm and the serial number of Ozzy Hidell's "MADE ITALY" rifle (C2766).

I drove carefully, within the speed limit, to Love Field. I located the area where I was to leave the car and, in the trunk, the duffel bag containing the morning's clothes, the set of identification for Mr. Graves, and the bogus Secret Service credentials. I parked right where I was supposed to, removed the other suitcase from the back seat, and locked the car. I placed the keys back on the left rear tire. Walking inside the terminal, I checked in for my flight. Everything was in order, as I knew it would be. Smith or his people would be picking up the car, disposing of the duffel, and sanitizing the vehicle somehow.

I had plenty of time before my flight to Los Angeles. Everywhere, it seemed, people were in shock at the assassination of John Kennedy. The announcement of the capture of Lee Harvey Oswald confused me. Who the hell was Lee Harvey Oswald? I learned Governor Connally had been wounded and a Dallas policeman slain, evidently by Oswald, as he attempted to elude capture. I wondered if Connally was hit by the last shot I thought I heard, right as I squeezed off the fatal round. I sat in the Dobbs House with a hamburger and a coke as I mulled all this over. I was surprised to find I had finished the meal with no memory of having eaten it.

Emotionally, I was on overload, my brain whirring disjointedly. Walter Cronkite's words replayed over and over. Only when I got on the plane did my mind begin to slow down. Sitting in this calm, orderly environment, listening to the comforting drone of the engines, I wondered: Had this all really happened? It seemed unbelievable, yet here I was, winging my way out of Dallas. I looked down at the city, and imagined I saw the chaos in Dealey Plaza. It was a surreal thought. I fingered the ticket envelope on which I had written the numbers that defined the fictional life of John Graves. I turned it over and discovered something odd: the ticket had been purchased in California. Stamped on the back of the envelope was -

All Points-All Ways Travel Service

The Man on the Grassy Knoll

13549 Ventura Blvd.
Sherman Oaks, CA
State 8-7760 or Triangle 3-2635
and, most peculiar of all, the penciled note -
PTY3

Party of 3? I got up and wandered around the plane, which was lightly loaded, looking for Mr. Smith or anyone else I might possibly recognize, although I didn't know who that might be. There was no one. Too tired to think about the ramifications of what I had found, I returned to my seat. As soon as we had established the operation schedule, Smith had perused the departing flights from Dallas for that afternoon and come up with two choices: L.A. or New York. Washington, D.C. or smaller cities were to be avoided. International destinations were also ruled out, as these could come under heavy scrutiny. Borders could be sealed. For the same reason, ground transportation to Mexico was deemed unsuitable. There was no real reason to leave the United States, anyway; assuming I got out of Dallas, Smith had said, virtually all the short-term danger would have passed. Besides, I had no more passport, although Smith said I could have another set of I.D., in another name, on a moment's notice. He hadn't wanted me traveling with any false papers out of Dallas, though, in case I was stopped for any reason. Logically, that made sense: if I was stopped at all, false identification could damn me, not save me. My own I.D. would be the only option. The only discrepancy was the airplane ticket - actually two tickets, on different airlines - in different names. As soon as I knew which flight I was taking, I would discard the other ticket. At that moment, an airport trash barrel had a perfectly good Braniff ticket to New York.

The Man on the Grassy Knoll

Both destinations were large coastal cities which would facilitate anonymity and, if necessary, the ability to disappear more readily. Scheduled departures would allow plenty of time in case of unforeseen delays with the mission. Braniff had a 1:30 pm departure for Idlewild, a late afternoon nonstop and one after midnight. I'd never have made the 1:30 plane, so that hadn't been considered. American flight #55 to Los Angeles wasn't much later than the second Braniff departure; it was six or one half dozen of the other. For a variety of reasons, Smith chose Los Angeles as the primary outlet but also procured the backup ticket for me - under a different name - on the Braniff red eye to New York, should things really go awry. The forecast weather in both cities was just a few degrees apart, and not too different from Dallas: between 55 and 60 degrees.

Anyway, all that was behind me. I fell fast asleep, emotionally drained and exhausted, winging my way toward the west coast and away from the gunfire in Texas.

Chapter 23

In Los Angeles, I stayed, ironically, at the Biltmore, site of the 1960 Democratic convention which had nominated John Kennedy for the presidency.

Along with everyone else, I was glued to the television once I checked in. When Oswald's picture first appeared on the screen, I realized he and Al 'Ozzy' Hidell were one and the same. Someone had used his head for a punching bag, and I really didn't blame whoever it was. The cop he'd gunned down on Tenth Street, who had stopped him as he fled the School Book Depository, was identified as an Officer Tippit. The poor guy had left a family. As I viewed, I picked up the hotel note paper and pen. I figured out the alias: LEe Harvey OswALD = AL HDEL = Al Hidell = Ozzy Hidell. It wasn't too tough.

I also learned the President's body had been taken to Love Field, probably right around the same time I arrived there. I hadn't known that, sitting in the coffee shop, and it was something we hadn't taken into account. It gave me an eerie feeling. It might have screwed up the departing flights, although mine was substantially later. Smith had been right about the Tex-Mex border: it had been closed, if only for a few hours.

By Saturday evening, I really didn't want to watch any more or have anything to do with it. I was in emotional shock.

The Man on the Grassy Knoll

I knew, though, it could be vitally important for me to know just what was going on so I forced myself to watch. It became clear that unless the police were misleading the press, the trail might stop with Oswald. I was, of course, worried that he would start spilling his guts and racked my brain to recall if I had given him any helpful information that could aid in identifying me. I didn't even know if Oswald/Hidell thought he'd fired the fatal shot; if indeed I had heard a third round from his rifle he may have thought he was responsible - he may never have known I fired.

When Jack Ruby gunned down Oswald on Sunday, I shook my head in disbelief. I had never heard of Jack Ruby. Was this a plot within a plot? It gave me a measure of comfort to know I had Smith's fingerprints tucked away in a safety deposit box.

Before the following week was out, I confirmed that a transfer of $75,000 had been made into my Bahamian bank account. I phoned my parents and told them I was changing careers. Not to worry, but I saw greater opportunity elsewhere. They were very understanding.

"You'll never get rich working for the government," my father said on the phone. Well, he didn't have the overall perspective, did he? He brought up the Kennedy shooting. Like everyone, he'd been stunned. Mom had cried at the news. He said how terrible it all was and that the country was headed to Hell in a hand basket. I forced myself to agree and changed the subject as quickly as I could.

My business with Mr. Smith had been concluded. Three lives had been taken: John Kennedy, Lee Oswald, and J.D. Tippit. Another, Jack Ruby, was in jail. The nation was in mourning. While the curtain was coming down on this tragedy, a new, darker age in America was dawning. The shots in Dallas reverberated throughout Dealey Plaza, the Texas landscape and across America. It would be decades before their echoes faded away.

Chapter 24

I didn't leave Los Angeles until the end of November. I wasn't really focused on my surroundings, so I didn't see much of the landscape. Mostly, I stayed in my hotel room and watched television, as the aftermath of November 22 unfolded. The events of that weekend were assuming an historical import. Somehow, when all the business with Mr. Smith had been ongoing, I had not realized this. It all just sort of progressed from one thing to another, under his control. In hindsight, it had been abstract, theoretical; Cuba seemed more an idea than a real place, a romantic, exotic idea, and the concept of helping overthrow an oppressive dictatorship a romantic notion. I'd almost been flattered to play a part. I *had* been flattered to play a part. Even when the target changed, I hadn't grasped the reality, really. I'd diminished the concept by personalizing it, romanticized the idea by linking the shooting to my friend and his sister. I'd made it small so I could grasp it. I'd been isolated, ungrounded, without friends, no one to jerk me back to that reality, no one to say what the hell are you doing? No one grabbing my shirt and saying Hey, pal, this is *real*.

And so now I began to have the eerie sense that I was a part of the history of the 20th century. Lee Oswald's life was chronicled and exposed to public light. Every detail was flushed out and examined. I learned Ozzy had a wife, a pretty

The Man on the Grassy Knoll

Russian woman named Marina, and two young daughters. The business of his dual home life became clearer. The marriage hadn't been going well – that was no surprise to me – and his weekday rooming house existence was not just for commuting convenience. A weekend dose of Lee Oswald would have been enough for anyone. Speculation that he may have been involved in an attempt on the life of a General Walker, at his home in North Dallas, was brought up. This ordinary whackball, this - I could find no better word for it - *jerk* - was now going to be in the wax museum line with Brutus, John Wilkes Booth, Leon Czolgosz, Charles J. Guiteau, and a host of other psychopaths who had slain a national leader.

And the thing was, he didn't really do it. At least, he didn't do most of it. No paraffin for Mr. Smith or me. The irony of it all.

The lowest point for me, of course, was the funeral. I don't know why the hell I watched it. The ceremony transcended the individual, so that regardless of President Kennedy's faults, bad judgment, reckless diplomacy, or, accepting Mr. Smith's argument, seditious actions, the leader of the free world was being laid to rest and virtually all the citizens of that international community were in mourning. It was as though the United States of America were being interred.

It was as though I was being interred.

The image that burned into my conscience was that of little John-John, standing at attention, saluting his fallen father as the coffin passed by. That gray and black specter, the quietly horrific image, became a firebrand on my soul, characterizing the magnitude of what we had done. What I had done.

The Man on the Grassy Knoll

I decided I was not a California person, although I had not done very much sightseeing. I had business in the Bahamas, eventually, so I flew east. I stopped off at my parents' house en route. That proved a big mistake.

My father picked me up at the airport.

"Sorry the job didn't work out, son," he said as we drove toward the house. "We were hoping you could stay for Christmas."

"Thanks, Dad," I said. "I'd love to stay, you know that, but I've got to start work in a few days. Really, everything's OK. I'm getting a lot more money."

I had told my parents I would be moving to Miami, where I had taken the position of magazine editor. The job required some travel, and I was going to be using my college degree. Cover stories came easily to me now. My mom cooked me a big meat loaf dinner, with mashed potatoes and gravy and peas and chocolate cream pie. All my favorite stuff. How sad, I thought. The more I looked at the food, the sadder I became. It was like the time, as a little boy, maybe in the second grade, I broke my crayons in some kind of angry fit. That memory, for some reason, was painfully sad. I couldn't really look at crayons after that. Now the meat loaf was the same way - somehow ruined. I ate all she served me anyway, of course, and I thought she hadn't noticed anything amiss. Fat chance. I couldn't fool my mother.

When she asked me what was wrong, I spun a tale about a lost love, using Mirasol as the mental model. I had fallen in love, and it didn't work out. Fiction came as easily as the truth.

"You'll get over it," she said. "There are plenty of fish in the sea." Good old mom.

162

The Man on the Grassy Knoll

I flew on to Miami the next day. I had tried my best, but the stopover had been a mistake. I knew my parents were concerned. I applied for a new passport, since I was no longer John Graves, and while I waited for it to issue I drove down to the Florida Keys. I had vague thoughts of going to Mexico or Brazil or maybe Argentina and brooding with the expatriates.

I still had a few hundred bucks of Mr. Smith's expense money. I stopped at motels in Key Largo, Marathon, and Key West. I took long walks on the coral sand and began drinking way too much - beer in the daytime and whiskey at night. The vision of the little Kennedy boy saluting his father's casket daunted me, from Los Angeles to Mallory Square. The thought of Christmas approaching was appalling. The days were bad and the nights haunting. The sunsets in the Keys, rather than displaying God's celestial palette, were but blood rust staining the sea.

I put off going to the Bahamas and collecting my $150,000. Instead, I went back the other way. Like a Bedouin, I crisscrossed the country, haunted by memories of Dealey Plaza and the funeral. I recall speaking to no one at all. People seemed transparent, insubstantial as ghosts. I flew to Phoenix and drove to Sedona, in the breathtaking high desert country of Arizona, where I had been profoundly affected by the peaceful surroundings. It was all so still. I desperately wanted to call Debbie, but I knew I was in no shape to see her. The vision of the Kennedy boy became unbearable. I had made those adorable children orphans, never to see their father again, never to receive his pats on the head, his hugs and kisses, never again to be graced with that famous smile. I had wrenched their family apart with violent death, turned that vivacious First Lady into a charcoal smudge, veiled in black,

163

draped in tragedy. I had made millions of women cry, shocked children into incomprehension, shattered a nation's spirit. Men had wept openly, stared in shock. My actions now seemed inconceivable, as though the past nine months had been a horrific *cauchemar*. The weight of it had come crashing down, almost a palpable thing, crushing me.

Finally, disoriented with remorse, blinded by guilt, sodden with alcohol, I made my way up a winding road to a beautiful, almost miniature church high on a bluff overlooking Sedona: The Chapel of the Holy Cross. Through the magnificent, tall glass window framing the cross I could see forever across the valley. It's where I met Father Donnelly. Kindly, graying, probably in his mid-sixties, with twinkling blue eyes, he could have been cast for the part. He had retired from his parish in Boston and was visiting the pastor, Father McNamara. He said he'd found the same pacific sense of calm I so desperately sought in that place.

Father Donnelly told me later he thought he'd seen a ghost when our eyes met in that sun-dappled place. He said it was as though the light avoided me. It was obvious I was someone in deep trouble. He reached out to me right then. This remarkable individual started me on the long road back. I wasn't even a Catholic, but I poured out my Confession to the priest; I knew he was bound to silence. I did it face to face because I didn't know how to use a Confessional. I suppose I expected him to recoil in horror, meeting a real life Judas Iscariot, but instead he reached out and placed his hand on my shoulder. I broke down completely. Great, wracking sobs reverberated throughout that little cathedral, like the gunshots in Dealey Plaza.

The Man on the Grassy Knoll

I had no place to go, really, and so Father Donnelly arranged for me to stay at a retreat site being put together by Father McNamara. I don't remember much about my surroundings, except that there were occasionally a few people around. I couldn't say if I communicated with them. I slept on a cot when I slept at all. Dreams melded into nightmares, blurred into wakefulness. It wasn't always easy to tell. My mind recoiled at any attempt at thought; I was paralyzed with a kind of shellshock.

Slowly, gradually, I unfroze. Over the next five weeks, Father Donnelly helped put the broken pieces of me back together again. I couldn't even tell how he did it, because I don't really know. Mostly, he listened as we walked among the red rocks, the desert willow and tall ponderosa pine. He tried to convince me that even I could be forgiven, and in the end I almost believed him. It was enough, I suppose. In February, I left Sedona to begin the task of setting down, in note form, all that had transpired since the spring of 1963. I would have liked to have remained in that quiet, beautiful place to set about the task, but I didn't want to overstay my welcome. My memory is, for things like conversations, very retentive, but I knew I needed the notes from my meeting in the Chinese restaurant with Mr. Smith and they were not with me.

It was not easy, but I needed to face everything head on, and I knew that I had to document the truth.

I was just about out of money by now, and so I finally went back to Nassau. I retrieved the $150,000 and closed out the account. The withdrawal limits Mr. Smith was going to impose were not in place. I was glad, by that time, the funds were in my name and I didn't have to live any more lies.

The Man on the Grassy Knoll

Maybe Mr. Smith had realized that - he seemed to know pretty much everything else. I tried, then, to get on with my life as best I could. It would be nice, I suppose, to say that I gave Mr. Smith's money to charity, or that I did some altruistic good works with the $150,000, but that would be less than truthful.

How does one restart a life after the cataclysmic events of 1963? Slowly, painfully, endlessly turning over the unanswered questions, seeking and not finding definitive answers, judging oneself again and again, but moving on nonetheless, as we all do, as the pain recedes, too slowly, and memories soften.

And that's how it was until Mr. Smith reentered my life: without warning, suddenly, on a sunny Saturday almost five years later.

Part II

1968

Chapter 25

I can't describe the three years following Dallas very well. Struggling in a murky soup, seasoned with the bitter herbs of self-loathing, I grasped for the feeble light above. My brain had numbed my torn emotions. Without Mr. Smith's $150,000, I don't know if I would have made it. Fit for no useful purpose, I thought about ending it all, but didn't have the courage to do even that. After a time, the task of documenting the events of 1963 occupied me. I hoped the act would be a kind of penance, purging, to some degree, my guilt: it didn't happen. It was, I think, more an act of self-flagellation. Neither did it afford any measure of clarity, as I said at the beginning, and as the reader can doubtless tell. There was no way to focus the diffuse light, no clear understanding of why I had done what I had done. I waffled back and forth. It seemed, on balance, an act of madness in a time of insanity.

After finishing the journal, I wrote and sold short stories and a few magazine articles. The writing was without depth. I reached out to a few old classmates and friends, but most had scattered before the turbulent winds that gusted across America during those years. Liaisons with melancholy, transparent women faded in and out. Thoughts of those sweet, eternally spring days back in college, playing baseball and living a carefree existence, were grotesquely impossible memories: sepia toned images from someone else's life.

My crutch for a time had been Father Donnelly. He'd been the only glue holding my soul together in that Arizona desert retreat. We'd kept in touch. He was ailing now, perhaps gravely. I flew to Phoenix and visited him in St. Joseph's, the Catholic hospital on West Thomas, with no purpose other than to provide whatever comfort I could to the man who had kept me sane. Yet he wouldn't hear of it; he only wanted to know about my welfare. Tubes and things were sticking out of him, he was running a fever, and he just wanted to hear how I was doing. I lied, and of course he knew it, and I concluded I was doing him no good at all. Afterward, I drove down Central the short distance to Madison, and the Sing High Cafe. I stopped the car and stared at the building. My appetite vanished. I didn't go in.

Before flying out, I looked in the phone book to see if Debbie was still at the same address. Her listing wasn't there. I dialed the old number, and someone answered in Spanish. It would have been nice to take her on another hike up Pinnacle Peak, maybe have another mesquite cowboy steak, but it wasn't to be. I had a couple of hours before I had to return to Sky Harbor, so I drove north to see if I could find the restaurant anyway. I took Seventh Street past Sunnyslope Mountain, but made a wrong turn somewhere, maybe on Thunderbird, while I was daydreaming. I wound up in Moon Valley, a lovely spot but nowhere near the Pinnacle Peak Patio.

I couldn't even get to the place alone.

From Mr. Smith, I had heard nothing, no word about my friend Ramon Figueroa, no communication of any kind.

169

The Man on the Grassy Knoll

Maybe Smith was involved in Southeast Asia along with just about everybody else, and I would be the last thing on his mind. Or perhaps I had served my purpose and been discarded. I could not even imagine in what foul enterprise he might be engaged. It was probably just as well.

By 1967 or so, after great effort, some measure of normalcy had gradually returned to my life. Like in all things, no matter how tragic, how devastating, the human spirit learns to cope with the cards that are dealt, or those it deals itself. There were periods when the events of 1963 did not occupy my mind: first hours, then days, then nearly a week. I had started a small business with a portion of the capital from Mr. Smith, almost as a distraction. I relished the mundane problems of a start-up operation. It surprised me by growing and becoming profitable. I dared to think I was on the road to healing and perhaps making something of the rest of my life. I was a million years old, and I was only 26.

On March 16, 1968, Robert F. Kennedy announced his candidacy for the Presidency of the United States. To me, the news was a lightning bolt, jolting the fragile world I had been slowly rebuilding. The implications were sinister. Didn't the man suspect anything? Was he writing his own death warrant?

I hadn't seen Mr. Smith in over four years, but I had little doubt he was still active. Men like Smith wouldn't just fade from the picture. It appeared the forces that aligned to remove the Kennedys in 1963 were still present. While Vietnam was a gaping wound, Cuba remained a festering splinter. The Mafia hated RFK's guts. The Teamsters wanted him drawn and quartered. Could the same thing happen again? Surely not. It would be impossible. Wouldn't it? Smith would be exposed, his cadre brought to justice. They wouldn't dare. Maybe they felt the threat had receded. Maybe Smith was sick, or dead, or involved with some other unimaginable project.

I almost believed it.

What should I do? Could I find Edward Smith, see what he was up to? Maybe he really was on the other side of the world, making his mischief somewhere north of Saigon. But if I found him here, then what? Stop him, somehow, if he was again on his murderous course? I didn't know. I knew I needed to try and locate him, in any event.

One step at a time. Not like Dallas.

Just like Dallas.

I took a breath, shook off the thought. Without his real name, I hadn't the faintest idea how to begin, and of course I would have to go it alone. I had no training in the art of being a spook except fabrication - Smith's admonition that a lie is mostly the truth, with the details left out. I'd gotten pretty good at it. I remembered the business card he'd shown me: an address on N Street in Washington. He'd also said it was an old card, and maybe it was. What could I do, go to D.C. and wander around N Street, looking for what? Smith to pop out of an office building at noon and go to lunch at a nearby restaurant?

And how would I stop him anyway? Certainly not with logic or emotion. I'd locked away the T48, and never fired a shot since. Was my jerry-rigged insurance policy, the glasses with Smith's prints on them, still any good? Did fingerprints last forever? I didn't know. These were crazy thoughts, I knew, but I thought them nonetheless.

It's all so difficult when you have to go it alone. How does one person balance a teeter-totter? For several days, I

171

discarded idea after idea, one half-formed plan after another. I was still nowhere when, on an ordinary sunny Saturday, the phone rang.

I hadn't needed to find Edward Smith after all; he'd found me.

Chapter 26

I was stunned to hear that familiar voice. He asked how I was.

"Okay," I managed.

"Good, good. I'd hoped you were doing well." Did he really think that was possible?

"How are you? Are you all right?" I had no doubt he was just fine.

"Sure." It was probably the most introspective statement he'd ever made.

"How'd you find me?" As soon as I asked, I realized how ridiculous the question was.

"Oh, you know. I still have a few resources." I'd bet he did. "Listen, if you've got some time in the next couple days, I'd like to meet with you."

I felt a shock. "What for?" I must have sounded pretty guarded.

"Well, you know, catch up on things."

Were we old fraternity buddies? My silence grew loud.

"Is that all right?" he asked.

All right? Nothing we'd ever done was all right. Why was I suddenly reluctant to meet with Mr. Smith when I'd been racking my brain trying to figure out how to do exactly that? But of course I knew why. I was pretty sure I knew what he wanted, and dreaded it. I knew how persuasive Edward Smith could be. Perhaps irrationally, I didn't want to give him another opportunity to sway me. Part of me was afraid that if met with him I might fall under his spell. Again. He would, I knew, make another effective presentation, weave his magic threads into a tapestry that could dazzle me. Somehow, he'd show me how only the two of us could save the world. Again.

But in the end it wouldn't work. Beyond anything he could say, above all that, Robert Francis Kennedy had ten children. The image of little John-John saluting his father's coffin had just about destroyed me. It remained a permanent imprint shadowing my mind. No matter what Smith could show me, no matter what he would say, that was overriding. I thought about Father Donnelly as well, lying on his deathbed, smiling his absolution at me through the tubes and monitors and paraphernalia of the dying. I didn't have to ponder any further.

So I would meet with my mentor again. I was making up my mind, perhaps without realizing it, that I was committing myself to stop Edward Smith.

And maybe I could get some answers to the questions that still whispered to me at night.

"John?"

"I can meet with you," I said. "Not here, though. I'm going to be in Las Vegas from Tuesday to Friday next week. Let's do it there." I would be attending a small business convention.

I was really uncomfortable with the notion of meeting Smith in my home territory. I suppose it would have felt as though he were desecrating it. Besides, let him expend a little

174

effort. We agreed he would phone me at a particular date and time in my hotel room in Las Vegas to set up a dinner meeting.

I was nervous, jumpy; after these convalescing years the past was coming back to life, without warning, without preparation, jarring my equilibrium. Aside from my fear the Kennedy candidacy was prompting our meeting, I was jittery anticipating the curtain being drawn back a little more on the events of 1963, and learning as much of the truth as I could. The burning questions had cooled to embers over the past four years, but now they flamed brightly in my mind.

I had one piece of information Smith didn't know about. It was my only card, and I'd have to choose the best time to play it. There was one thing I needed to find out. If indeed Smith was on another recruiting trip, I had to try and determine if he was the last link in a long chain or the key force behind his cabal. If the former, and somehow I neutralized him, it would probably make little difference. There would simply be another Edward Smith to take his place. Well, maybe not as formidable a personality as Smith, but there would be someone. It was a daunting thought.

I'd booked into Caesars Palace, which had recently opened. The gigantic hotel was like nothing I'd ever seen. My bed was on a dais, with curtains all round. It looked like a bordello. I'd heard the ceilings were mirrored, but that wasn't the case, at least in my room. I sat in an armchair, nervously awaiting his call. The phone rang at the appointed time and Mr. Smith suggested an Italian restaurant I had patronized during a past trip. The food, I knew, was first-rate and service excellent. The guy still knew where to eat.

A taxi took me over to the restaurant, by the Flamingo, and there he sat, at a quiet table, waiting for me. He smiled and waved. As I walked over, he stood up and we shook hands. It all seemed so *ordinary*, and that made it so extraordinary. My mind was awhirl as this living reminder of the turbulent past stood in front of me. Smith had aged well; there was still the lean, agile look that radiating vitality. I had pegged him at perhaps 40 when we had met in 1963, but that may have been on the long side: he didn't look a day past that age in 1968. The hair was a bit longer, tinged with gray, and maybe he had edged up to 200 lbs, but the immaculate white shirt and erect bearing were the same.

There was a long silence as we faced each other over our drinks. It is impossible to explain the emotions that ran through my mind as I studied him, the same half-smile playing across his face, the familiar appraising look. Things really hadn't changed that much at all, it appeared, even to the martini that sat in front of him, or the Bloody Mary, complete with celery stalk, next to me - just as they had for our first meeting five years earlier, in another restaurant, another life. Time seemed to fold over and almost touch itself. And yet this could not be so. As I sat there, emotions tumbled through me like tangled clothes in a dryer. I have no hope of explaining this to the reader, but even after all that had occurred, and all that I feared might yet occur, one of the emotions was a kind of strange affection, probably like a private toward his lieutenant who had led his company on a bad, casualty-filled mission, and yet both had survived. Or perhaps the inexplicable bond that can form between captor and prisoner, kidnapper and victim. Or maybe as two divorced people, after the tumult and acrimony, meeting for a drink long after the sounds of battle and discord have died away, with no more scores to settle, no more wars to be fought, only the faded glow of the good times. It made no sense, but I found myself calming down.

Try as I might, I could not hate this man, whom, I had come to realize, had been as a surrogate father for a time. I feared it would make my task all the more difficult, if Smith was here for the reasons I suspected.

But then again, I'd done this all before, hadn't I?

How does one begin a conversation like this?

With the mundane, it seemed.

"How are you, John? You look well," he said.

"I'm pretty good. You look pretty good yourself. Still keeping fit, I see."

"I do try," he smiled.

Somehow, for a moment, with one part of my mind, it was as though those years had melted away, and I was a kid just graduating college again. It went on like this for a couple of minutes, awkward yet not uneasy, until I told him that while I did not know the purpose for which he had called me, I wanted answers to many questions. Smith nodded.

"Well, of course. I owe you as much. That was one of the reasons for calling you. I'll tell you what I can," he said. "But let me ask you something."

"What?"

He signaled the waiter for another round, although I was only half finished. He leaned forward.

"What we did – I know it came at a cost – but what we did very likely saved millions of lives. I want to know if you believe that."

I was pretty sure where this was going, now. I was surprised he'd brought up the subject so soon; Smith sure didn't leave his kings in the back row. In order to learn his plans, it would be vital to appear I'd bought into the program, that I could still be a viable asset. If I told the truth, I'd never know. This would be our last meeting.

I sighed. *A lie is mostly the truth.*

"I won't say the cost wasn't great. You know it must have been. But I believed what you told me then and I want to believe it now. That's why I need some more answers."

Smith looked at me closely. "Yes," he said finally. "We're unsung heroes, then, aren't we? There is a great sacrifice in that."

Virtue is its own reward, I thought crazily. He must really believe it.

"I never heard from you about Ramon Figueroa," I said. I tried not to sound accusatory. I had to play this right, this balancing act.

"That's because there was nothing to tell. I kept my word. We went through back channels, everything. Nobody knew anything."

"You could have told me you struck out," I said, a bit testily. "You knew how important that was to me." I wondered if he was telling the truth.

Smith just shrugged. "I probably should have. I figured you knew I'd contact you if we found out anything."

"Before Dallas, I'd asked you if there would be a change in Cuban policy with a new administration."

"We've done as much as we can. Most of the changes are behind the scenes, mostly because of the Cubans in Miami. They're nuts and they're very vocal. Somehow they've got hefty clout in Washington. It's pretty complicated. Now everything's about Vietnam, anyway." I figured that part was probably true. The waiter brought the drinks; I drained the rest

178

of my Bloody Mary and handed him the empty. We watched him leave.

"Well, the first thing I want to know is what happened to that authorization form I filled out and the secrecy agreement," I asked.

"They were removed and destroyed as soon as I could retrieve them," Smith said.

"Okay," I said. "Good."

It was better than good. I had a whole mental checklist of questions, but I didn't get past the first one.

"Listen, John, before we get too much further along, I need to tell you the main reason for this meeting."

There was a silence. He focused on me intently. For a moment, I felt like an insect, pinned to the cloth. I reminded myself this was not 1963.

The moment passed.

I heard my own voice. "Well, as soon as RKF announced his candidacy, I wondered if the phone would ring."

Smith nodded. "Let me say this straight off. If you don't want to be involved, you won't be involved. You've proven yourself already. I know I can rely on you, so you're the first choice. But if you want out, so be it."

If I want out? Just like Smith. The question assumed I was already in. I nodded.

"I want to ask you something," he said. "Do you still have the two glasses with my prints on them?" Oh boy, that was an ominous query. Was he saying this on purpose, right now?

Of course he was.

The Man on the Grassy Knoll

"Yeah, in a safety deposit box, just like I told you back then." So there.

"You really did save that stuff?" he smiled. "I thought maybe you were just bluffing."

"Doesn't really matter now, I guess," I said. Nothing could be further from the truth. "How about you, did you forget to put the withdrawal limits in place?" I asked. "On the $150,000, I mean."

"I know what you mean. No, I didn't forget. I knew there was no worry there so why hold any of it up? It was probably going to be safer just letting you get it all at once. I knew you'd be careful with the money, keep it under wraps. You earned it, anyway," he shrugged.

I must have still been a bit nervous. I found I'd gulped half my second Bloody Mary already.

"Listen," I said, "you're going to have to justify this. There has to be a compelling reason and I don't see it. Cuba's not on the front burner anymore. It's all southeast Asia. "

"Nothing could be further from the truth."

"What do you mean?"

"Who do you think was responsible for most of the Cuba mischief during JFK's administration?"

"You're going to tell me Bobby Kennedy."

Smith leaned in and spoke with intensity. "Absolutely. Let me tell you what the reality is. Kennedy thinks Dallas was a Castro operation. He'll stop at nothing to avenge his brother's death. That's half the reason he's running."

"What?" That was a staggering statement. Could it be true? "Where the hell did you get that?"

"You forget what my job is. This is what I do."

180

The Man on the Grassy Knoll

I really needed to keep my wits about me, and the alcohol wasn't helping.   I had thought to keep Mr. Smith oiled, as I knew from past experience his tongue would loosen. The problem was, though, mine was starting to thicken. I was getting a buzz. We needed to eat.   I looked around, but our waiter must have been in the kitchen.

"What evidence does Kennedy have that Dallas was a Cuban operation?"

"Evidence?   What, are you kidding me?   We *manufacture* evidence. He doesn't need evidence. He hated Castro's guts even before Dallas. Since when does evidence have anything to do with anything?"

"What are you talking about?"

Smith looked at me as one would an infant. I hated when he did that.

"Think, John. Evidence is just stuff you make up to tell the public why you did what you wanted, or to get people to do whatever you need. We do it all the time. It's called disinformation. Those guys did whatever they wanted to do and made up evidence later. You already know this. Look, when Stevenson was humiliated in front of the U.N., trying to say Cuban emigrants had been behind the Bay of Pigs instead of us, he was using fake CIA photographs. I told you that before. It was all in the papers."

Had he? I didn't think so. *Fake CIA photographs. To get people to do whatever you need.*   Smith had shown me CIA "evidence" before Dallas, hadn't he?

"You showed me those ship photographs."

Incredibly, Smith just nodded. Then he breezed right by. He ticked off items on his fingers. "The fake Cuban defector pilot was exposed because his plane still had wet paint markings on it. The Joint Chiefs wanted to blow up one of our own battleships in Guantanamo Bay and blame it on Castro. We made Cuban army uniforms -"

"What?" I interrupted. "No one would believe that about the battleship, for Chrissake."

"It's true. Bobby Kennedy gave the plans right to Lansdale."

"Who's he? Is he a CIA guy?"

"Edward Lansdale. CIA field commander, former Major General, came up through OSS. Not someone you'd ever want to meet. He's black ops personified. Ruthless, lots of stories about the guy. Needless to say, he was ready to run with it."

My head was spinning, whether from the alcohol or Smith's allegations. Or maybe both. Somehow, another round of drinks had shown up.

"You said Bobby Kennedy was the main force behind all the Cuban stuff. You're going to have to give me examples."

Smith nodded. "I'm prepared to do that."

"Go ahead."

But he didn't.

Chapter 27

"All right," Smith said, sitting even straighter. I could see him mentally rubbing his palms together. "I'm going to assume you're onboard, unless you tell me different." He looked at me, eyebrow raised.

What? I hadn't meant go ahead, like go ahead with the plan. I meant - damn, this wasn't going like I intended. This wasn't at all going how I needed it to. The guy just kept coming. What had made me think I could control a conversation with Edward Smith?

"I'm going to assume you're onboard, unless you tell me different."

Hadn't he just said that?

"Right."

"Right, you're onboard, or right, you understand?"

"I understand," I said. I'd just have to be flexible and bide my time as the evening progressed, it seemed. People were being seated at nearby tables as the dinner hour got into full swing. There was plenty of ambient noise, though, and Smith must have been confident no one could hear.

He nodded. "Okay. First, there's no assurance Bobby's candidacy will be viable, anyway," he said. "He'd have to take the nomination away from Johnson. That's pretty tough, trying to knock an incumbent out, but he is a Kennedy. Nothing's going to happen unless he's got a real shot."

No pun intended, I thought. "Well, that makes sense."

"Secondly, we've got a huge advantage over 1963. There's no Secret Service protection. He's just a candidate."

"I guess that's true." I hadn't thought about that. He was a United States Senator from New York, and I had just assumed he'd have some protection from somebody.

"What do candidates do? They go everywhere, give speeches, press the flesh. They're totally exposed. No doubt Bobby will have private bodyguards, but that's window dressing."

I felt a chill. For Smith, this would be duck soup. "Go on," I said.

"Plus, we've got lots of time. There's no time pressure. So here are the questions: do we wait until after the convention in Chicago? Like we said, he might not even be nominated. It'll be an uphill fight."

"When is that?" I asked. I didn't follow politics. At least, not anymore.

"Late August. Presumably security will be tighter if he wins the nomination. Now that's not a real worry, but it is a consideration. Secondly, what environment do we want? Outdoors, like Dallas? Indoors? If it's inside, there are lots of attractive options. All these guys use back stairways, freight entrances, employee entrances, kitchens, to get in and out. Those are can't miss opportunities, but not as easy to slip away. Outdoors, we already know about. We need a marksman, but getting away's much easier."

He looked at me, as if for confirmation.

"If it's indoors, you're right. You don't need a rifle unless it's a large auditorium or something. You wouldn't need me."

184

The Man on the Grassy Knoll

"We'll use the same basic set-up."

"Same set-up? What do you mean?"

Smith looked at me as if to a small child who couldn't grasp basic arithmetic. "Two shooters, of course. A patsy with a cheap popgun and the real shooter."

"What?" is all I could manage.

"It worked before, didn't it? It worked perfectly. Who's going to tamper with success?"

A proven formula. Time-tested. Jesus Christ.

"Don't you think – do you really think you can get away with that again? What, another Warren Commission deal?" I asked.

"Use your head, John," he said. "Of course we can. Who's to stop us?"

Who's to stop us? My God. Had he really said that?

There was a candle burning on our table. I hadn't noticed it before, but they'd just dimmed the lights for dinner. The place had a pleasant atmosphere. For some reason, I thought of Mirasol. It would be nice if she were on the other side of the table. We'd never gotten the chance. I wondered if she was safe, and what she was doing now. I wondered again if I ever crossed her mind, if she'd ever tried to contact me.

My thoughts floated to Debbie. It would be terrific to have her on the other side of the table, candlelight flickering off her soft, blonde hair. I couldn't imagine her married. I should have kept in touch with her, at least.

Both had vanished, though, hadn't they?

"Speaking of money, here's the deal."

Had we been speaking of money? I didn't recall that. Maybe I'd drifted for a moment. I took a breath and refocused.

The Man on the Grassy Knoll

"It's the same," Smith continued. "A hundred fifty thousand, half in advance, offshore account, just like before. All right?"

Of course, the question assumed I was in. I knew I wouldn't be committed until Kennedy proved a viable candidate, anyway.

"When? I assume any payment wouldn't be until after Kennedy's candidacy looks like everything's a go."

"That's right. Okay. Let's talk about the weapon. Do you want a T48?"

Do you, not would you, he'd said. Mr. Smith was moving right along, wasn't he? Evidently the Russian window dressing was no longer a factor.

"For outdoors. Yes, I think. The scope was just right for Dallas."

"You were unbelievably close in Dallas." That was true. "Let's eat."

Smith signaled for the waiter. He arrived in a moment. I hadn't seen the guy in fifteen minutes, but Smith conjured him up with a wave of his hand.

As we ordered, another server topped our water glasses and left a small plate of garlic bread. There was a spot of red sauce on his white sleeve. I munched on a slice. It was delicious; the crust was crunchy and the bread soft and warm, with just enough garlic.

By now the place was crowded. This was one of the quieter restaurants in Las Vegas, but even so the level of background conversation, the rattling of silverware and clattering of dishes had increased. It was not unpleasant. The patrons seemed festive and enjoying themselves. Maybe most of them hadn't hit the casinos yet. There were lots of attractive women, perfectly coiffed and dressed to the nines.

Our food arrived surprisingly fast. · In this town, they wanted you back on the gaming tables, pouring money into the drop boxes. Our conversation meandered as we ate. As I remembered from my previous visit, the spaghetti and meatballs were delicious. We talked about lots of things; we talked about nothing. The major league baseball season: could Jim Lonborg repeat as Cy Young Award winner? The upcoming Oscars: would *The Graduate* take Best Picture? Italian food. Las Vegas architecture, if that's what it was. As I had come to expect, Mr. Smith never said a word about himself.

We were sipping double espressos when I gathered my resolve. I couldn't let Smith's sleight of hand take me off my main focus. I'd never find the pea in this deadly shell game.

"I haven't said I'd do this yet. I need you to take me through Dallas."

Smith's sigh said do-we-have-to? I tried to look implacable. Some seconds ticked by. I watched a busboy clear a table. Silverware rattled; glasses clinked. I imagined the distant clashing of swords.

"All right." Smith settled himself closer and began:

Once Operation Kidron was born, and my target diverted from Castro to President Kennedy, Smith said he used his access to classified material to set up the machinery in Texas. He had knowledge of the parade route well before the newspapers published the information. That brought us to Lee Harvey Oswald. Where had he come from? Was it really coincidence that Hidell/Oswald began working at the School

The Man on the Grassy Knoll

Book Depository in October? Was he truly set up to run interference, take the fall, become the patsy for the operation?

Smith said Oswald really fell in his lap from another agency source, although the ex-marine was really just a name and a file. This created a minor problem, as the other agent was not involved in Operation Kidron and Smith had to take responsibility for Oswald with some delicacy. He said Ozzy was regarded as a loose cannon, a nut case, and from time to time had come under the purview of both the agency and the FBI. Although at that point a domestic issue, his prior travel to Russia had created a file in the CIA. Smith also told me that Oswald was the shooter who fired on General Walker through his window, which I already knew, as it had been well publicized. I recalled Oswald had elaborated on that story to me. Although he had hinted at a clandestine operation, the reality was the Walker incident was no one's idea except Oswald himself. At best, he was deemed someone to watch and possibly control on a low level. Otherwise, he was just another whack ball.

"Whose idea was it to use Ozzy in Operation Kidron?" I asked.

"Mine," he replied. "I had full field responsibility for all operational phases of Kidron, without the need for prior approval on anything. The opportunity was too good to pass up. He didn't need much impetus."

"Who did he think you were?" I asked. I recalled Oswald's strange remark to me about Smith and his credentials. It had been evident to me he had thought Smith was other than CIA.

"Soviet intelligence," he replied. "I told him KGB would get him to any country in the world he wanted. He'd be

188

a Hero of the Soviet Union. Set him up for life. No more work, no factory job in Minsk. He didn't need much of a push."

Smith picked up his drink and sipped. Suddenly, I had a crazy thought. What if Smith really was KGB, and I was the guy who saw the phony credentials? Then maybe Bobby Kennedy was right, and Castro had been involved in Dallas. It seemed pretty unlikely, but then again it kind of fit, didn't it? I thought back to the manual I'd found in Smith's trunk, and the stupid meeting I'd attended back at the Copper Tankard. Was I on to something? Maybe up was down, right was left, and maybe I'd really fallen into the rabbit hole.

I'd seen *The Manchurian Candidate*, the Oscar-nominated film. Sinatra had been surprisingly good. Was I Laurence Harvey, the brainwashed Communist tool?

But then again Smith had supplied Soviet weaponry. He wouldn't have done that if he really was KGB. Still...

I took a deep breath. Another piece of string leading into the tangled ball of yarn. I'd have to think more about it, when vodka wasn't fueling my thoughts.

Smith brought me back to the present.

"Tell you the truth, I don't think I had to offer Ozzy anything once I planted the idea in his head. Those crazy eyes lit right up."

I knew what he meant. I had looked into those same eyes. "I'll bet you had the credentials," I commented. Now I had more than a passing interest in his answer.

"Sure I did," Smith said. "Of course."

"And the job at the School Book Depository?" I asked. It couldn't have been more perfect for the operation. Oswald had told me he started there in October.

189

The Man on the Grassy Knoll

"Dumb luck. Fate. Call it what you will," Smith replied. "I had nothing to do with it. How could I? He got the job in October. It really was an amazing stroke of luck," he said.

"I suppose I don't have to ask why you didn't supply him with a weapon?"

"You know the answer. He was strictly on his own. The whole thing fell together like a perfect jigsaw puzzle, didn't it? Like it was fate."

By design, Oswald was not provided with an escape route. He had little or no money, no expense account, and had to bum rides, travel by bus, or hoof it. His intelligence and attitude lent him as a foil, a scapegoat for the mission. If he were caught, he was a dead end. That was why Smith never wanted us to meet, but I had insisted.

"Weren't you worried if he were caught? You told him you were KGB," I said.

"So?" Smith replied, "You had a Soviet weapon. The primary goal was to divert suspicion from within. That would have been catastrophic. All other options were tolerable."

It had the ring of truth, I decided. I wasn't Laurence Harvey, and I hadn't been a tool of the KGB. I almost felt relieved.

"Anyway, it was immaterial. He'd never have told," Smith continued. "You heard him, sized him up. He kept asking for a lawyer, and the cops ignored him. He wanted F. Lee Bailey. He'd have gone to his grave first. That was my judgment."

I thought about it, and had to agree. Oswald/Hidell would never have told them about Smith. It wouldn't be in his code of behavior.

190

The Man on the Grassy Knoll

In truth, he *had* gone to his grave first.

"I was surprised he got as far as he did," Smith said. "I wouldn't have bet he'd have gotten out of the building."

Smith knew who would fire first, shooting from an exposed position, and likely draw a response. The concept that Hidell/Oswald might actually hit his target with a twelve dollar mail order toy was just an unexpected bonus.

It was all just as I had thought.

"And Ruby?"

Smith looked me straight on. "We never heard of him. Unbelievable, wasn't it?"

Yes, it was.

Something important had nagged at me, something I hadn't realized until months later. I'd wondered about it since, and it might have some bearing on what I needed to know.

"Oswald could have talked, even though I agree he probably wouldn't have. They could have found the Tokarev. How could you know you weren't going to start World War III?"

"It's amazing, all they got was his lousy Italian rifle. It was all kind of ordained, it seemed."

What an incredible remark, I thought. Maybe Smith thinks of that day as some kind of divine, wonderful operation. That was what was amazing. He was right, though. It did seem unworldly, the way it all dumped out right on Oswald's head. The poor, dumb bastard.

"I wondered if you were going to ask me that, back then, but you never did."

"I guess I wasn't that smart back then. You know that already, anyway. How could you be certain we wouldn't retaliate?"

The Man on the Grassy Knoll

There was a pause. Smith looked at me.

"I was certain. It wouldn't have happened."

I looked hard at him.

"It was under control," he said evenly.

I thought for a minute. That could only mean one thing. How high up could this go?

"The motorcade," I said. "Johnson was there. He was right there." Was he ready for any eventuality? "There was a judge to swear him in. The machinery was all set, wasn't it?"

"Don't jump to conclusions," Smith said. "I'll tell you right now, he wasn't involved. He was accessible, that's all. Judges are everywhere, anyway."

Accessible by whom? Who could have engineered that? And that judge was a Kennedy appointee. They weren't everywhere. There was one last piece of the puzzle.

"What about the Warren Commission?"

"What about it?"

"How did you know they wouldn't uncover anything?"

"Are you serious? Nobody was worried."

"Why? Did you have any influence over the Commission?"

Smith smiled. "Of course not. Why would we? The government was running it."

Chapter 28

"Okay, let's get back to business," Smith said.

"Let's take a walk," I replied. We'd been sitting, it seemed, for hours. I needed to stretch. Although it was only around 7:30, I was a little groggy with the time change and pasta; the espresso hadn't kicked in yet. Mr. Smith suggested we take the short walk to the Flamingo and continue in the lounge. It was late March; the air was cool, eddying around us in a slight breeze. It brought the musty smell of desert dust.

As we strolled along Las Vegas Boulevard, I reflected that it was now five years since I'd first met this man who'd completely changed my life. What was five years, the wooden anniversary? Maybe he should give me a pencil. Maybe it was paper, I didn't know. Boy, I must be in a fog, I thought, to be thinking these stupid thoughts. I had to sharpen up.

So I'd peeled back the first layers of the onion. The conspiracy had gone high enough to control foreign policy. Smith had been given full autonomy for Operation Kidron. I still needed to know the extent of the conspiracy, if his cabal was firing up again. We entered the Flamingo, which was pretty crowded, maybe because the marquee was advertising Duke Ellington's band performing in the Driftwood Lounge. It wouldn't be conducive to conversation. Smith ordered a martini and we strolled around the gaming floor for awhile as the heavy meal digested. I'd seen *Viva, Las Vegas* with Elvis and Ann-Margret, filmed at the hotel. I didn't recognize anything, though. We paused at a craps table where some guy was betting a hundred dollars on the Pass line. Onlookers oohed and aahed as he won and lost. We drifted on. Eventually we found an alcove with comfortable chairs near the lobby. We sat catty-corner to each other; quite close. It was fairly quiet. No one was near.

"Look," Smith said. "You wanted examples about Bobby Kennedy before committing. I'll give you some highlights, like a Readers' Digest Condensed version, okay?"

"Okay." I hadn't realized we were in a hurry.

"Back then we had Project Rifle, a bunch of active assassination squads, and they were run in parallel. I didn't have much to do with that. I was peripherally involved with Operation Mongoose."

"What the hell was that?" Talk about drama. These guys had code names for everything, it seemed. Probably lunch, as well.

"Originally, a bunch of low-level, conventional ops against Cuba. Textbook stuff. For awhile, Lansdale ran it."

I never had a textbook like that in school, I thought.

"There were these two guys in Mongoose, Hawkins and Esterline. Bobby Kennedy wanted to ramp things up and so they planned, basically, the entire Bay of Pigs operation with Brigade 2506. The whole thing was a real growth industry. The Kennedys put tremendous pressure on us, on everybody, about Cuba. They were nuts about Castro. He thumbed his nose at us every time we screwed up. Nothing seemed to work. Bobby bugged everybody all the time, pissed off a lot of competent professionals. All the intelligence services became his play toys, pretty much on a daily basis, especially after all the ops kept getting screwed up. What they didn't know was that Cuban intelligence had infiltrated the organization."

Faintly, I heard an excited roar from the casino floor. Somebody's ship had come in.

"What's Brigade 2506?"

"Brigade 2506 was a bunch of Cuban exiles training for the Bay of Pigs in Guatemala. We ran the thing. I mentioned them before, when you were trying to find your friend."

It must have gone right by me then. "Was Ramon Figueroa or his dad members of Brigade 2506?"

Smith shook his head. "No. We don't think so. We tried to check it out. The Brigade sailed from Nicaragua, anyway."

I thought about that disastrous invasion. "I guess you guys didn't do a very good job. The invasion, I mean."

"You don't think so? Somebody leaked the plans to the press. That was two days before the operation. Kennedy, John Kennedy, froze up; he couldn't decide. He let the invasion occur, but without vital U.S. air cover. It was an irrational act. The landing force was cut to pieces without air support. Kennedy was to blame, not us. I told you this already, before Dallas," he said.

I'd investigated his story back then and confirmed it. But now Smith was backing off his claim that President Kennedy leaked the invasion date. Over the years, I'd suspected as much. Incompetence was not the same as culpability. I was also becoming convinced the whole sideshow with the Soviet warships, the pictures I couldn't decipher, had been manufactured.

The Man on the Grassy Knoll

It's called disinformation. We do it all the time.

"Back in Eisenhower's administration, Ike issued something called Directive 5412, which forbade the use of our armed forces for clandestine ops. Hawkins and Esterline came up with the crazy idea that if the invasion force established a beachhead, we could recognize them as a provisional government and could then send in our troops."

"It sounds nuts," I said.

"It was nuts. Here's what you have to understand, why this thing needs to get done. The whole concept was based on an idea, an idea still prevalent in the agency even today. The thinking is that if our covert ops could ignite a spark, the general population would rise up against Castro. It's crazy. The guy's more popular than ever at home but they're blind to it. In Miami, the Cuban community is even crazier. Alpha 66, Veciana and those guys. They're very vocal and demonstrative. Don't think that doesn't influence our people. And Bobby Kennedy knows it. He probably believes it too. He's a match to a powder keg."

"What's Alpha 66? Sounds like a highway." What a convoluted tale.

"Ex- Cuban military organization, mostly in south Florida. They're a pain in the ass, really."

I shifted in my seat. Five years ago, I'd have been drawn in to the drama, hanging on every word. I was still drawn in except that now I knew what he was doing.

Smith continued. "Bobby Kennedy was the main cheerleader for the whole thing, inciting everyone, pushing everybody. Much more so than Jack. After the Bay of Pigs disaster, after RFK took over Mongoose, they even drew up plans for a second invasion, AM/TRUNK. It was

The Man on the Grassy Knoll

unbelievable. Those six nuclear-tipped missiles with Cuban fingers on the triggers, the ones that would have started World War III, had no effect on the White House. We were going to send 100,000 troops onto the beaches. They would have been eggplant."

A gaggle of showgirls strutted by, laughing and chattering. For some reason, they looked sexier in street clothes than they would half-naked on stage. Smith didn't seem to notice. He looked off, shaking his head slowly.

"Anyway, instead of scaring the crap out of the administration, it had the opposite effect. Like I said, Bobby Kennedy took over Operation Mongoose. He was driving everybody nuts, especially Edwards."

"Who?" I asked.

"Sheffield Edwards. Head of Security. Edwards was the guy who suggested the whole Castro assassination deal anyway. He gave the job to Bob Maheu, a bagman for us. Maheu got $150,000 from the company to pay for the Castro contract."

So. That's where the money came from. "My hundred and fifty."

Smith nodded. "Yeah. It was on the shelf when I needed it for you. It was supposed to go to AM/LASH, but he became unavailable."

"AM/LASH?" Christ. You can't tell the players without a scorecard, I thought.

"Yeah, another operative. Rolando Cubela. You really filled a need, thank God."

So now he was thanking God. I supposed he would. Smith was citing more names, being much more specific than he'd been in 1963. Perhaps he viewed it all as ancient history,

197

but it implied a degree of urgency. He knew he had to assuage my guilt, reinforce the justification for what we had done in Dallas, romanticize the killing, all the while shifting the blame to Robert Kennedy, making him the warmonger, the fanatic. Smith was cementing the foundation so he could build to the next level. He didn't know I was already there.

Damn. The guy was good, though.

Chapter 29

I looked at my watch. I hadn't changed the hour hand. It was only nine o'clock here; midnight at home. I was, I realized, exhausted.

"Here's what I think. Before we wrap this up, I need to sleep on it. But I also know I'm dead tired now. I've got a seminar at eleven tomorrow. How about we get together before that?"

Back in my room, I reflected on our meeting as I lathered in the shower. Smith had been unusually candid, but I hadn't fully achieved my objective; I still didn't know the scope of the operation. Some of what he'd said was so strange, it seemed unlikely he could make the stuff up and expect me to believe it. His approach was more matter-of-fact, more conspiratorial, than before Dealey Plaza. I had the eerie feeling history was repeating itself. It was really unbelievable. My only advantage was that I'd been here before. Smith had kept his end of the bargain years ago, depositing the rest of the funds in my Bahamian account, but I doubted he'd really made much of an effort to locate Ramon Figueroa after telling me Abelardo was dead. It seemed as though he was taking my demeanor at face value. I hoped I'd struck a believable balance between caution and – what – loyalty? A belief in the cause? It seemed, in his eyes, I was a proven member of the shadowy conspiracy.

199

The Man on the Grassy Knoll

In fact, I *was* a proven member of the shadowy conspiracy.

I fell asleep immediately: without dreams, I think, and slept for nine hours. I hadn't done that since – I didn't know, maybe before Dallas.

We met in the Caesars coffee shop at eight a.m. Of course, it was really eleven for me so I was hungry and well-rested. My brain felt reasonably functional. We were seated right away in a booth to the side; no one was near. As usual, this stuff seemed to work out for Mr. Smith. Since I'd first met him, we'd always gotten together in public places. I hadn't really focused on that, but now it could be important. I imagined it was part of his modus operandi. I supposed they all did that. If things played out like they might, I would have a problem in a public area, wouldn't I?

I went for the southwestern omelet with hash browns and bacon. It might have been a holdover from my time in the desert with Mrs. Dell. Mr. Smith ordered the same.

"Are you staying here?" I asked. He shook his head, pointed a finger vaguely.

"Up the road." I guess that was standard practice also.

"What time's your flight out?"

"One something."

The food arrived. We both laced our meal with hot sauce. The omelet was delicious; the bacon crisp and tasty. Las Vegas food was really good. And cheap. We busied ourselves eating for a few minutes.

Afterward, we sat with our coffee.

"This is pretty good coffee," Smith observed. "You know, I kind of like this town."

The Man on the Grassy Knoll

"I liked it since I came here in the summer of 1963. Remember?"

"Sure I do. You drove up from Arizona."

"Yeah. I lost a hundred bucks at the craps tables, as I recall."

He signaled for the waitress. As always, we got instant service and she refilled our cups.

Smith leaned closer. "Okay. I'd like to finalize this."

It was time to play my only card. "In a minute. I need to ask you about something. Let's talk about Task Force W."

Smith actually blinked.

"What?" He'd heard me, all right.

"Task Force W," I repeated. "DFG."

"What do you know about Task Force W?"

I shook my head. Uh-uh. I wasn't going to play that game. "Wrong answer."

Smith stared at me. He leaned back. Once before, I'd seen his wheels turning, when I'd told him about my stash of drinking glasses. They were whirring furiously now. Then he nodded, as if to himself.

"Okay. Task Force W was our outfit in Miami, one of our locations in Miami, that ran a bunch of Cuban ops back then."

"What kind of ops?"

"Cuban stuff. Same crap. None of it worked either."

"And DFG?" I didn't know if DFG was a person, place or thing, so I kept the question vague.

"Des FitzGerald. He ran the operation for awhile."

"Did you know him?"

"Sure. I liaised with him. He made a career out of failed assassination attempts on Castro."

The Man on the Grassy Knoll

I carefully tried to steer the flow toward the conspirators, where I had been trying to go the previous night.

"Did you have autonomy to recruit me, or did you have to go through FitzGerald?" I was afraid the question was too direct, but it didn't seem to bother Smith. Maybe he thought he was talking about ancient history. Maybe he was comfortable now with the thought we were teammates again.

"I had complete autonomy for the operation. FitzGerald had no involvement."

I tried again. "Was there a specific incident that changed my target?" It was an oblique question. What might lead to why, why might lead to who.

"Specific incident. Yeah. Absolutely. June 19, 1963. That was the date that finally sealed it."

"What happened?"

"You have to judge this against the backdrop of the missile crisis and how close we came to a nuclear exchange then and at the Bay of Pigs. Despite all that, on June 19, JFK issued a memo authorizing further ops against Castro. His brother had drafted it. He was escalating the whole thing again. It was all fun and games to those guys. Another touch football game with the nuclear football. That's when we finally realized it was never going to stop."

There it was. *We.*

"And then what?" I felt my pulse increase.

"You know what. Operation Kidron."

We were closing in now. "How did it happen?"

"What choice was there? JFK wasn't the main problem, so taking out his brother was the first consideration. But that didn't really solve things completely. Neutralizing the President would automatically get rid of Bobby too, end the whole damn thing. Even though Kennedy's popularity was sinking, the next election was too far away. So the decision was made. No one could have imagined the situation now. Who in their right mind would have thought Bobby Kennedy would run for Jack's job?"

Maybe no one in their right mind. "Who made the decision?" I asked.

Who was behind it?

Who dreamed up Operation Kidron?

Who ordered it?

Who knew about it?

Who knew about it and could prevent United States retaliating against an alleged Soviet operation?

"I'd like to move on now," Smith said.

"If you answer that question, I'll tell you how I know about Task Force W and FitzGerald."

Smith looked at me for a few moments.

"All right."

"Who made the decision?" I repeated.

"It's not all that clear-cut," Smith said.

"No. Don't give me that." I said.

"What I mean is, it evolved as kind of a joint thing. In the end, it came from two people. And they had to tell a third, to be sure. Me. But one gave the order. Directly."

"Just two people did this?" Somehow, this hit me right in the breadbasket. "Not a whole - consensus?"

"Five people did this. Me, you, Oswald, the other two." I was speechless. Smith had created the impression that just about everyone was behind Operation Kidron. I suppose it had stayed with me like a childhood myth, over the years, as a measure of comfort. But it never would have worked, I realized. With a group, the truth would have come out a long time ago. I pondered this for a few moments. I had a lot to think about. Maybe this could really be stopped.

"Don't look so stunned," he said. "That's four more than the Warren Commission said. I don't even know who the other one was. All I can do is make an intelligent guess. I just know who gave the order, because he gave it to me in person."

"Are you going to tell me who it was?"

"You can make your own intelligent guess."

That was it, then. That's all it took. Not a big quorum, not a consensus - just one or two people to change the nation's history. My God. It really was unbelievable, wasn't it?

I'd gotten my answer, learned what I needed to. *Maybe I really could stop it.*

"How do you know anything about Task Force W?"

"When I drove Ozzy out to get his rifle," I said. "I looked in your trunk. The file was in there."

Smith smiled and nodded. "The infamous white Impala. Find anything else?"

"A manual. Some type of manual about dress codes, tipping, etc. It was marked up. I guess it was a guide for your agents."

"Aah, yes. That book's still in the field. Load of crap, really. Learn anything?"

"I learned about raincoats," I replied.

"I told you once before you had a future with us," he said, with a suggestion of a smile.

"I've got my seminar pretty soon," I said. "Let me mull this over until I get home, all right?"

"You want to think about it for a few days?"

The Man on the Grassy Knoll

"You said we had plenty of time. It's not like buying a car, for Chrissake."

Smith looked thoughtful. "Sure. Think this over for a couple of days. I hope you're onboard, but if not, I'll need to find somebody. It's up to you, okay? I'll phone you after you get back home."

We shook hands; Smith was not one for long good-byes.

205

Chapter 30

After my seminar, I ate a leisurely lunch: BLT on white toast and a chocolate milkshake. I would have shot a little craps, since I didn't have another meeting until three. My mind was elsewhere, though, lost in thought as I drained the last of the shake. It was delicious, rich and creamy with a nice glob of ice cream at the bottom of the glass. I needed some exercise; I'd probably put on two or three pounds since arriving in town. I took a brisk half hour walk down the strip and got rid of that logy feeling.

I went back upstairs, took out a yellow pad and made notes. The first thing I wrote down was that I really had no assurance Smith represented the same people as he had in 1963. After all, as I'd realized earlier, Bobby Kennedy had lots of enemies. The man was intelligent, yes. But he was brash, cocky. As Attorney General he'd gone after the Teamsters, hounded the Mafia, tried to desegregate the government. If Smith was right, there was no love lost for RFK in the clandestine services either, and they'd be the ones with the best opportunity through Mr. Smith. Cuba was still Castro's dominion, but the tension had receded considerably. There was no guarantee Bobby Kennedy would ramp things up again against that country. America was certainly in no mood for further foreign hostilities; Vietnam had been enough of a

The Man on the Grassy Knoll

wrenching upheaval. Besides, Kennedy had given fiery anti-war speeches in the preceding twelve months.

Smith could be fronting for any number of groups, really. I'd believed the man in 1963; I'd become convinced we were headed into nuclear war. I still believed we were at terrible risk then, even more so after what I'd learned from him over the past twenty four hours. Of course, if elected Bobby could reignite the stealth war against Castro, renew the assassination attempts, especially if he thought the Cubans had a hand in his brother's killing. The public wouldn't know.

Smith had made another effective presentation, but I was a little older and hopefully wiser.

As I gazed down at the Grand Canyon on the flight home, I reflected. Was my reasoning sound, or was I grasping at redemption? Was this to be my penance? Would it be enough? Maybe I should I just say no and walk away. That certainly was the easiest option. Could I just walk away?

I didn't know all the answers, and maybe I never would, but there really was no choice. I had to try and stop this. The thought sickened me. Dealey Plaza had almost destroyed me; I'd had enough violence for a lifetime. I prayed Kennedy's candidacy went nowhere.

Declining to participate wouldn't be enough. For this operation, Smith had lots of time and didn't need anybody who spoke Spanish. For $150,000, he'd find a marksman, all right. There would be no one to help me, no way to involve anyone else without condemning myself. As always, over the past five years, I was alone.

Five years ago, I had been in for a penny. Now I was in for the pound.

The Man on the Grassy Knoll

I considered my options. If the plan went forward, Smith and I would probably travel back to the Bahamas as before, depositing the $75,000 advance. There would be plenty of opportunity to – to neutralize him at that time. It couldn't be in Nassau, though, because I had no legitimate way to take a weapon through Customs.

The desolation of Arizona would be perfect, except I doubted I would be training in the desert again. I was rusty, but I still knew the T48 backwards and forwards. All I needed to do was brush up at any local shooting range. It would have to be Miami, before we boarded the plane for Nassau. Or, come to think of it, after we returned. If I waited until the actual mission, I had no way of planning my actions.

Back home, I was busy with work for the next couple of days. There was nothing much to do, anyway, except begin to formulate a plan and monitor Kennedy's campaign. I half-convinced myself that RFK would have no chance for the nomination against the incumbent when, on March 31, President Lyndon Johnson stunned the country by announcing he would not seek re-election. What had been speculative was now probable. I felt physically ill, powerless against what now seemed some malevolent inevitability. Was everything about all this preordained? How could this be?

Again I knew despair. I breathed formaldehyde and not the flowers that had just begun to bloom again. I was caught in an endless dance with death; the darkness that had fallen in 1963 had again come crashing down, and all my efforts to lift it during the past five years had been in vain. I knew what was coming.

And I had to stop it.

Chapter 31

Four days later, on April 4, Martin Luther King, Jr. was gunned down on his hotel balcony in Memphis. I was as shocked as anyone. I doubted Mr. Smith was involved. While King had been a charismatic leader and hero to the integration movement, he had no real power and there appeared little pragmatic value in eliminating him. I was following RFK's campaign, hoping without much hope it would tank. The Senator had given a speech at Notre Dame that day, and another at Ball State, as the Indiana primary was a month away. He was getting an awful lot of media coverage and I knew he had a good chance of upsetting Eugene McCarthy, U.S. Senator from Minnesota, who'd been campaigning from the start. Supposedly Kennedy had asked McCarthy to withdraw when he decided to run. The egocentricity of that act boggled my mind. The Nebraska primary would follow a week later. These would be key battles in anticipation of the California race to be held June 4. If RFK continued gathering momentum, the phone might ring earlier than I thought.

Actually, it rang that evening.

"Hello, John. What did you decide?" So much for small talk. Smith didn't even mention the King shooting.

"Count me in," I replied, deliberately freezing my brain so I couldn't think about the words.

The Man on the Grassy Knoll

"Okay, good. There's been no decision yet, but it looks like the guy might make it." Smith sounded keyed-up, as though his favorite team was about to win the pennant. "I'll be back in touch as soon as we have a green light."

Adrenaline, or whatever it was, coursed through my veins. I held up my hand, surprised it was steady. I had taken the final step, the irrevocable decision committing me to stop Mr. Smith. There would be work to do.

On April 27, the ball game changed again. Hubert Humphrey, Vice President, announced he would run for the Democratic nomination. Despite being too late to enter any primaries, the press reported he was now the favored candidate. I breathed a hopeful sigh. With primary results see-sawing back and forth between McCarthy and Kennedy, the Democratic delegate count was fractured. Humphrey's nomination seemed more likely. I dared hope my business with Mr. Smith would be moot.

Smith's next call, then, was a shock. The date was May 15, the day after Kennedy, to my dismay, had taken the Nebraska primary and one week after his upset victory in Indiana. He was still trailing the Vice President by a considerable margin, though, according to the pundits.

"Time to saddle up," Mr. Smith said. "I'll be in town tomorrow." He named a large resort hotel a few miles away. "Can you meet me in the lobby, say ten a.m.?"

It wouldn't have occurred to Mr. Smith that I might have a life somewhere. "Sure."

"See you then." This whole thing had become an emotional roller coaster.

It was raining when I awoke, a steady drizzle that must have started hours earlier because the ground was saturated.

210

The Man on the Grassy Knoll

Puddles reflected the streetlights that were winking off. As I ate a bowl of cereal, I watched the morning news. Some low-lying streets were awash; the reporter said to allow an extra fifteen minutes for the morning commute. There were terrible pictures about a series of killer tornadoes that had touched down the previous night, mostly in Iowa, killing over a dozen people and injuring hundreds. It wasn't a great way to start the day.

At 9:50, I swung into the long hotel driveway and around the covered entranceway to the valet. The self-park area wasn't very far but it was still misting. I took my ticket and entered the lobby. The hotel had long, wide corridors with gilded ceilings and artwork throughout. Tourists in casual dress occupied several of the intimate seating areas here and there. Some were waiting out the weather in golf clothes or tennis outfits. I spotted Smith in an overstuffed chair, dressed in casual clothes, in keeping with the surroundings. He could have been waiting to tee off. He stood and waved me over. We shook hands.

"Hi, John. I've been here before, maybe twice," he said, gazing around. "This is a great place, isn't it? You ever come here?"

"Yeah, once in a while," I said. I'd played several rounds of golf and a few tennis matches at the facility over the last couple of years. Dinner now and then, but it was pretty expensive. "When did you get in?"

"Last night. I think Pahlavi stayed here a while ago." I guess he meant The Shah of Iran. He was the guy who had that good looking wife, Farah Diba, who reminded me of my mom. "Let's go upstairs. I've got some stuff for you." He led me towards the elevator.

The Man on the Grassy Knoll

His room, on the fifth floor, was actually a small suite. The nightly rate was probably quadruple the government allowance, at least. The furnishings were tasteful, perhaps Louis XVI, although I wasn't an expert. The pastel walls and Oriental rug cast a warmth throughout the room. A sitting area overlooked the central courtyard. The rain had stopped, I saw, and the air had been washed clear. The sun dappled the foliage, sparkling with drops. It was very pretty. We sat in two armchairs; there was a briefcase on the small, marble-topped table between us, resting on top of the New York Times. Mr. Smith leaned forward and snapped open the spring clasps. He took out a packet and handed it to me.

"What's this?" A sheaf of papers: the top page was a statement from my old Bahamas bank. "Isn't this premature? Humphrey's still the favorite."

"Success is when preparation meets opportunity, John," he said. Boy, there was a phrase. "I reactivated your old account. There's a card with new codes and instructions like before."

That was a surprise. "We don't have to go to Nassau?"

"No, no. Tomorrow I'll arrange the transfer by phone. I still know some people there," he said with a grin. It was nice to know I'd have another windfall, but it meant I wouldn't be alone with Mr. Smith in Miami. I would need to revisit my plans.

Smith swiveled the open briefcase around. "This had to be hand delivered," he said. Inside was a holstered pistol, a long tube and a cigar box. The tube must be a suppressor, I guessed, although I'd never seen one before. He handed the weapon to me.

212

The Man on the Grassy Knoll

"What's this?" I asked.

"In case we're indoors, like we discussed. A Nagant revolver. It's an interesting sidearm."

Indoors was high risk, despite Smith's apparent nonchalance earlier. Not that I was actually going to do it. Anyway, I'd never heard of a Nagant handgun, although I recalled the Mosin Nagant rifle in the desert. I extracted the weapon from its holster and hefted it. It felt light.

"What caliber is this?"

"7.62 millimeter." It *was* light. Why was I being given a gun like this?

Safety first. I flipped open the gate and rotated the cylinder. The Nagant held seven rounds. The chambers were empty.

"It's not loaded," Smith said.

"You have to load this by hand? One by one?"

"How else? It's a revolver. You can't change out the cylinder. See the ejector rod under the barrel? Unscrew it and it tilts out. It lines up with a chamber so you push the rod back in and knock out the casings after firing. It was ridiculous under combat conditions because it was so slow. But that won't matter for you. You're not going to be in a firefight."

He was right, but not for the reasons he thought. There was a big Soviet star on the revolver, just like on the Tokarev. It looked even older than the rifle, maybe from the Revolution. The star was big enough.

"If it's so crummy, why are you giving it to me? It's just another Commie gun, isn't it?" I said.

"It is a Russian weapon, but that's not the main reason you're getting it."

The Man on the Grassy Knoll

The holster wasn't even a shoulder type. The pistol had a lanyard and was obviously military. How the hell would I wear it? The weapon seemed inadequate.

"What kind of holster is this, anyway? I'd look like a Mountie, for Chrissake. This is ridiculous." What the hell was going on? I was starting to get agitated. Was I to be the patsy this time?

"Hey, hold on a sec. Don't get excited. Listen, they don't make a shoulder holster for it. It just comes like that, military. But here's the thing. It's the perfect assassination weapon. I'll show you why." Smith said. He opened the cigar box, which held maybe three dozen rounds. I picked one up.

"What is this?" The ammunition looked a little odd. Actually, it looked a lot odd. The cartridge shrouded the whole round, so it looked like an open lipstick tube. The bullet was deep inside. It was the weirdest thing.

"Well, it's 7.62mm, like I said, but it's dedicated. You use that special ammo for this pistol."

So that's it, I thought. They wouldn't need the gun to trace it to the good old U.S.S.R., just a round of ammunition. Clever.

"Look at this," Smith said. I was curious about this oddball weapon. He gestured and I handed it to him. He cocked the hammer.

"Yeah, it's double action. So what?" I asked.

He shook his head. "Look closer," he said, relieving the hammer. "Look at the cylinder when I cock it."

As he cocked the hammer again, I looked as directed. The cylinder rotated and moved forward against the barrel. "See that? Know what that does?"

I had no idea. "No."

214

The Man on the Grassy Knoll

"It drives the neck of the cartridge into the forcing cone and creates a seal so no gas escapes. Very efficient. No other gun in the world does that. That makes it about the only revolver that can take a silencer, except maybe the model 10 the Seals are getting in Vietnam."

"What? Why?" I didn't quite get it.

"The brass seals the bullet, and the cylinder moves forward and seals the barrel. No gas escapes and it boosts muzzle velocity. Perfect for a silencer."

I picked up the suppressor and hefted it. It wasn't that light. It looked like a one-off.

"Custom job?"

"Our own design. State of the art."

"Pretty quiet, eh?"

"Dead quiet." I caught the irony.

"The Nagant can actually take .30 caliber ammunition, but then it couldn't be suppressed," Smith continued. "The Russians used this as their main weapon of assassination. Some V.C. have it now. When you fire it, all you hear is the click of the hammer. Get it?"

Now I got it. I had never seen anything like that before. Smith told me the revolver had been designed in the late 1800's by the Nagant brothers, a couple of clever Belgians who went on to design automobiles.

"The Russians bought tens of thousands for general field use," Smith said.

"The cars?"

Smith gave me a pained look.

"So would the – the patsy guy have the same thing?" I asked. "I guess not."

"Hell, no. He'll have something really loud." His eyes narrowed in thought for a moment. "Actually, that's an idea. The best thing might be the same pistol without the silencer."

"Do you know who he is yet?"

Smith shook his head. "It's going to depend on where. If we can use a local, so much the better. Then it'll look like a crime of opportunity."

Just like Oswald.

"What about crossfire?" I asked, as though I was really going to go through with it. "This other guy can't be opposite me, can he?"

"No, he can't. It will have to be carefully orchestrated, I know that. The last thing I'd want is to put you at risk."

Was he kidding?

I inspected the weapon further. The barrel was threaded for the suppressor.

"You've got a local range, right?" Smith asked. "Someplace to shoot the pistol?"

"I guess." I hadn't fired anything since November 22, 1963. I hadn't planned on ever firing anything again, but the music just went on and on.

"I couldn't get as much ammunition as I wanted before I left," Smith said. "It's not very common, as you can imagine. Think you've got enough?"

"I'll let you know," I said. "I see the serial number's been scratched off, most of it. Is this a registered weapon?"

"No, not at all. It's untraceable. The gun came that way."

216

The Man on the Grassy Knoll

"I wonder who used it, then," I said. "Somebody didn't want it traced."

Smith shrugged. "Some Bolshevik, maybe. Tell me what you want to do about the rifle, the T48."

"What do you mean?"

"You'll need to practice, won't you? It's got a four power scope. I know you know the T48, but you'll have to dial in the sight and practice with the actual weapon."

"That's right. So you didn't bring it?"

"Couldn't, I flew in. We'll relocate it when we pick the target site and you can get it fine-tuned in a day ahead or so. Or do you want to make a special trip?"

"Will you be there?" I asked. If he was going to be at the range in Arizona, that might be my best opportunity.

"No reason to."

"Okay, I'll wait until we know where we're going. I'm sure you can set something up."

Smith looked at his watch. I recalled his timepiece from five years before, with the expensive band. Maybe it lasted forever.

"Listen, can you give me a ride to the airport?" he asked. "We can have lunch here first." Smith always knew where the good food was. "My flight's around 2:30."

"Sure," I said. He nodded, got up and headed for the bedroom.

"Great. I'm going to hop in the shower and change. We can meet downstairs in ten, fifteen minutes or there's the paper, under the briefcase, or you can turn on the TV."

Suddenly I knew what I needed to do. Right now.

"I'll read the paper," I said.

"Okay. See you in a few." He closed the door.

217

The Man on the Grassy Knoll

Perfect.

Chapter 32

Slowly, deliberately, I picked up the pistol and the suppressor. Carefully, I screwed the device in place, ensuring I didn't jam or strip the threads. When it was finger tight, I swung the gate open, reached into the cigar box and inserted a cartridge. It fit perfectly; the round slipped right in. I rotated the cylinder one click and repeated the process. As I continued loading the weapon, I mentally reviewed who in the hotel had seen me with Mr. Smith. I was satisfied we had interacted with no one. By the time I had all seven chambers filled, I thought I heard the shower water running.

I held the pistol in my right hand, aiming it toward the window. Outside, it was impossibly bright. *Just like Dallas.* The suppressor's weight wanted to tilt the weapon downward. My left hand grasped my right wrist for support. I peered down the elongated barrel and saw that the Nagant was steady.

The walls were not painted, I realized; they were wallpapered with a light fleur-de-lis pattern. Very nice. Faintly, I thought I heard the curtain rings pulling along the metal rod. Smith was in the shower. I stood up and walked slowly, lightly to the bedroom door.

I suddenly remembered I'd valet parked my car. I cursed my stupidity, although I had no way to know I would wind up with a silenced weapon, alone in a hotel room with my quarry. Now I could be recognized; I will have transacted with the valet. There would be a delay waiting for the vehicle to be retrieved. Maybe they kept track of cars by license number. What else?

I'd hoped the door was maybe slightly ajar but it was closed. I had a sudden wild thought. Suppose this was a set-up? A true test to see if I'm committed? Smith had left me with a silenced, untraceable weapon and ammunition. We were alone in his hotel room. What if the shower was running for my benefit, and he was waiting on the other side of the door, firearm in hand, waiting for the knob to turn and me to slip in? What if those strange looking cartridges were really blanks?

Now my heart began to pound. Mr. Smith was not stupid; he didn't make mistakes like this. He didn't make mistakes at all. What was I going to do? I stood motionless with indecision. The room's tasteful décor became an incongruity.

There was no choice. I would never get another chance like this.

I knocked softly, then, holding the weapon behind my back, without a clear idea what I'd say if Smith answered yes? or opened the door. There was no response, but then again there wouldn't, would there? I carefully grasped the door handle, took a deep breath and turned it slightly. To my horror, it seemed to spring open with a click. I pushed the door slightly until I could peer into the room.

He wasn't there. Now I heard the sound of the water clearly. It varied as Smith moved around under the spray; he was definitely in the shower. I moved rapidly across the room to the bathroom door, which stood ajar. I took a quick peek. The bathroom was quite large. Through a veil of steam, his

The Man on the Grassy Knoll

shadow moved behind the curtain. I didn't know how long I stood there before I raised the Nagant toward the specter beyond the mist. If I fired through the curtain, I wouldn't actually have to see him.

And, as a wave of nausea washed up from my belly, I had an instant of clarity: John Fitzgerald Kennedy had never been a real person to me. I'd never seen his image except through a lens, whether television or sniper scope. He'd been a celebrity, a papier-mâché cutout, not real but a target, an electronic paste-up, a two dimensional cathode ray image, a print from Life magazine. Larger than life, and therefore not life. That's what was different now. Smith, to me, I suddenly realized, was a living breathing person, with all his faults, all his charisma: a life I had experienced, and interacted with, a human being. Unless I fired through the curtain, *right now*, I would have to do this infernal deed face to face. His eyes would lock onto mine after he stared down the silenced barrel of the Nagant assassination pistol. Would I waver then?

I stood motionless, took a breath and let it half out, cocked the hammer. The cylinder advanced, pressed against the barrel, just as Smith had shown me.

I squeezed the trigger.

Click. The sound was quiet as death, hardly audible above the stream of water. There was barely any recoil. The curtain rustled, jumped as the 7.62 round punched through.

Only drowning would be more silent.

He was still standing, moving. I cocked the weapon again; fired twice more. I heard what sounded like glass breaking. The acrid smell of gunpowder mixed with the rising steam. Three holes had ventilated the curtain.

What?

The Man on the Grassy Knoll

He was still standing. I rushed forward, flung open the cloth. My mouth fell open. Hanging from the shower head: a hotel laundry bag, and a towel knotted underneath. It moved this way and that under the jets of water, a faux Mr. Smith. Beyond, the shower wall had three shattered tiles; I was lucky I wasn't hit by a ricochet. I gasped and whirled around, four shots remaining in the Nagant, and rushed back into the bedroom. The closet door was open, now: was it moments ago? There were no clothes hanging, no suitcase in the room. Keeping low, I darted to the doorway, scanned the sitting room. The briefcase was gone. Mr. Smith was gone. There was nothing.

Chapter 33

My heart slammed against my chest wall as I rode the elevator downstairs. My legs felt as wobbly as pipe cleaners; I leaned against the side of the car. I fought the impulse to run to the front entrance. It seemed an hour before the valet retrieved my Plymouth. It took about as long to stop hyperventilating. As I waited by the curb, I felt an electric tingle, perhaps in anticipation of a bullet slamming into me at any moment.

I drove aimlessly, recklessly, barely knowing where I was. After a couple of miles, I pulled into a shopping center, checking my rear view mirror to see if any car had followed me. None that I could see. I parked in the middle of a row and turned off the ignition. My brain was on fire, neurons whirling at about the speed of light. I took a deep breath and sat for several minutes, willing myself calm.

What had happened?

I pieced it together. Smith must have seen right through my act in Las Vegas, or at least had doubts. A supreme judge of character, he'd realized I wasn't fully committed. This whole thing had been a test, a set-up, leaving me alone with a weapon, silencer and ammunition, presenting the perfect opportunity to remove him. Just as I'd thought, poised to open the bedroom door.

The Man on the Grassy Knoll

It was brilliant. If I'd headed down to the lobby, or just sat and watched TV or read the paper, he'd simply have emerged a while later and we would have gone downstairs to lunch. His confidence in me would have been reinforced. He must have been in the bedroom closet, and when I passed by and into the bathroom he slipped out the door. No wonder he hadn't yet deposited the $75,000.

Why hadn't he taken me out? Surely he had a weapon; the plan might have gone awry. Of course, I had a weapon, too, and was a crack shot – or at least had been, five years ago - so that may have given him pause. A primary reason I was still alive had to be the pair of drinking glasses locked away in my safety deposit box. Smith had asked about that right away. I had no illusions it was because of our relationship. I didn't know if he'd come up through the action services or not, but he certainly seemed capable. I already knew he was ruthless. The secondary conclusion was that he didn't need to remove me anyway, which meant there was no way I could interfere with his plans for Robert Kennedy.

But I couldn't rely on this logic. If I was wrong, I'd be dead wrong.

I had to act as though he either didn't care about his fingerprints or didn't believe I really had them. Maybe he'd never been printed anyway. I had to assume he'd just give the order, whenever he felt it convenient, and he was many miles away. Then I'd never know what hit me. Smith didn't do his own dirty work, as Ozzy and I could have attested. Why should he? He had the time and the resources. The risk would be someone else's.

What now? The first question: could I go home? Was I safe? The probable answer was yes, since I'd gotten out of the hotel without incident. Smith would know I was armed and on high alert.

I drove home, furiously trying to think. It was difficult, my jumbled mind still awash in adrenaline. I'd been shocked, scared, once again three steps behind Mr. Smith when I'd thought I was ahead. The Nagant, silencer still in place, sat on the passenger seat next to me along with the cigar box of ammunition. I tried to work out a plan. I entered my apartment cautiously; there was no one there, no one nearby. Then I sat down at the kitchen table and thought some more. It appeared I was out of danger, at least for the moment. The window of safety might be very small; things may have already been set up. I would be at risk at least until Bobby Kennedy either lost the nomination or his life. As soon as either occurred, I would simply be irrelevant, a dead end. I could go nowhere with what I knew. I should be safe, no longer a threat.

Should be.

But I really couldn't assume that either. I already knew Smith disliked loose ends. Despite what he'd said, Jack Ruby had been an awfully convenient coincidence.

The life I'd cobbled together in the last few years was finished. I would have to disappear. I closed my eyes. The adrenaline had drained away, leaving an empty, hollow feeling. Once again, I would have to start over. It was all so – endless. I felt a great tiredness, as though my bones themselves were exhausted. I must have sat there, motionless, for at least fifteen minutes.

But I had to get moving. My second in command, a bright, hard-working guy who'd graduated college two years prior, was fully capable of running my small company. I phoned and gave him a favorable buyout price, alluding to a health crisis in the family. I didn't tell him the crisis was probably going to be mine. I made a list of things I needed to do before leaving. By 3 p.m., I had withdrawn all but a few dollars from my bank accounts and taken the proceeds in cash. The amount was substantial; I ignored the questioning looks during the twenty minutes I was there. I got my T48 out of storage. It felt strange but comforting to heft that rifle again. Military holster or not, I wore the loaded Nagant as I packed up my possessions. That evening, the pistol rested on the night table as I slept.

In the morning, I rented a U-Haul trailer to tow behind my 1967 Plymouth Fury. Both were loaded by lunchtime - action allowed me the luxury of not thinking. I met my employee and we executed the purchase and sale agreement. I negotiated his cashier's check before the banks closed and was gone before the rush hour, out of town for good. It was all a wrenching experience but I tried not to dwell on its emotional impact. Or maybe I was just numb.

As I drove, I thought about the mechanics of a acquiring a new identity. I remembered asking Smith about it when we had gone to Nassau with my new phony I.D. a million years ago. I'd learned some useful things from my mentor. It was time to put some of them to work against him.

Chapter 34

It took me two days to reach my destination; I'd picked a small city with a desirable climate and good airline connections. I checked into a hotel and placed most of my stuff in a storage facility. Things would have to be on a temporary basis until I established a new identity and the Kennedy nomination played itself out. After a fitful night, loaded Nagant on the nightstand, I drove another eighty miles to drop off the U-Haul in another city. I wasn't going to leave an easy trail for Smith to follow. I returned in the early afternoon, with plenty of time to visit the main city cemetery and wander around until I found a grave that met my criteria: John David M___, born in 1943, had died in 1944. I began the task of assembling my new personage, applying for a duplicate birth certificate, social security number and driver's license. At least I would get to keep my first name again.

I'd remembered Smith's advice years ago about how to travel invisibly, and was pretty sure I'd left no clues. I had paid cash for everything. The only link now was my car, and I would sell it soon enough, but not in the same town. By lunchtime the next day, with most of my housekeeping done, the tension had eased a bit. I began to feel reasonably secure. It was a balmy day and I went for a walk. I found a pizzeria a couple of blocks from the hotel and thought over the situation as I ate a couple of slices. Before the bathroom incident, I'd wondered if I could I get up the courage to stop Edward Smith. That was no longer a question; I'd fired the Nagant through the shower curtain after only a moment's pause. I wouldn't hesitate again. I'd been trained too well.

Now, Smith and I might be stalking each other.

The Kennedy nomination was still in doubt, but the feeling of inevitability was strong. There were two watershed events looming. In just over a week, on June 4, the South Dakota and California primaries would be held. The Democratic National Convention began August 26 in Chicago; I'd checked the date. No one would know Bobby Kennedy's travel schedule after California, I reasoned, since he probably didn't know it himself; it would depend if he won or lost. I realized, then, that Mr. Smith could only pin down those two locations and dates for the foreseeable future. Realistically, the odds were long on finding Smith. But I'd know where his target was. My only hope would be to get close and locate the shooter. Shooters. There would be two, I was sure. I would have to go to California, and then to Chicago if Kennedy won. I supposed he could monitor the results from somewhere else, but I assumed Bobby would be stumping for votes in that critical west coast primary right up until the polls closed.

The next day, I brought my T48 and the Nagant to a local firing range. It didn't take long to get dialed back in with the rifle. I was satisfied with my shooting after the long layoff; the gun seemed kind of like an old friend from a past life. In a way, that was a scary thought. Had this become my true calling? I hoped not.

It was a far cry from pitching for the Yankees.

I shot the Nagant without the suppressor since I didn't know if the device was legal without some kind of permit.

The Man on the Grassy Knoll

The trigger action was horrendous. I estimated the pull was over ten pounds. Realistically, the gun needed to be cocked to fire without breaking a finger. The pistol was loud. I was amazed at the difference without the silencer. When it was attached, one could fire the Nagant in church and cover the sound with a cough. Yes, it truly was a weapon of assassination. Smith had said the V.C. was using them in the jungle. I wonder how many of our soldiers had been taken out in silence. It was a grim thought. I shot the handgun sparingly since I hadn't yet located a source for the odd ammunition.

I laid low for the next several days, waiting for the California primary. With time to spare, I resumed thinking how to go on the offensive. I made a list of all the people I could remember Smith having mentioned since Las Vegas. They sure as hell weren't the church choir. Could I somehow contact one or more of them, try to learn anything about Edward Smith's real identity? But how could I possibly do that? It seemed absurd. And even if I could, these people would blow holes in any cover story I could dream up.

I backtracked to the All Points-All Ways Travel Service in California, the outfit that had procured my ticket out of Dallas five years ago. That proved another dead end. The Texas license plate on Mr. Smith's car – PJ*8611 – was equally untraceable. I didn't even bother with the John Graves passport or social security numbers. I knew they'd been cooked up in the same clandestine kitchen.

The only clue might be something Smith had taught me years ago. If he'd followed his own advice, his real first name might be Edward. He'd described an Edward Lansdale, who seemed to be an awfully scary fellow. Could Smith be Lansdale? Probably not, or he'd have never mentioned the

229

guy. The CIA didn't provide a list of employees for me to peruse, either. Frustrated, I turned my attention back to the task at hand.

I decided not to bring the rifle to California. I realized I would have to stay as close to Kennedy as possible, and that would mean I'd only have the Nagant. If Smith was going to use sharpshooters, snipers from distance like in Dealey Plaza, I'd never be able to find them.

But I'd have to try. On June 3, I flew in to Los Angeles, armed with the revolver, phony business cards and press pass identifying me as a reporter for the New Orleans Times-Picayune. I'd done the cut-and-paste job myself, and it didn't look too perfect, but I figured no one would be scrutinizing the document. I encased it in old, cloudy plastic and then it looked almost real. The Louisiana paper seemed a good choice: well-known, not too small, not too large, not too close. I sure as hell hoped I didn't run into a real reporter from the Times-Picayune, though. I wasn't that good a liar.

As I had predicted, Senator Robert F. Kennedy was still in town. If I could pull it off, if I got lucky, if I didn't waver, we'd all have a final rendezvous.

Chapter 35

Tue June 4 7:49 pm

I have learned Senator Kennedy's plans only hours before I must leave to get to his location. He will be at the Ambassador Hotel, on Wilshire Boulevard, to monitor the California results. I take a taxi from my motel – most of the better hotels are full – over to the Ambassador around 8 p.m. The polls are just closing.

The place is huge, 500 rooms I'm told, and it's shaped like a gigantic sideways letter H, with a grand entrance in front. I'm wearing a sports jacket to cover the Nagant. I've purchased a shoulder holster instead of the ridiculous military job that came with the gun. I expect no trouble with access, thanks to my training with Mr. Smith; I can spin a story with the best of them. But I don't need to. I never even have to show my phony press pass. Everyone and everything flows freely from one part of the hotel to another. Security is, as far as I can tell, nonexistent. I am fearful that if Smith makes his move tonight, there will be little to stop him. Except maybe me.

I talk to other reporters, supporters, hotel employees. The press generally agrees Kennedy has been gaining momentum and has a good shot at defeating McCarthy tonight. I fervently hope not. The results are trickling in; the race is tight. It will be hours, then, before a winner is decided.

The Man on the Grassy Knoll

The New York reporters are all buzzing about a triple play the Yankees pulled off last night against the Twins. Baseball. The subject jolts me. The game might as well be on another world: unreachable, unimaginably distant. If I had never met Mr. Smith, I muse, maybe I'd have been watching from the bullpen.

What the hell has happened to my life?

I shake off the thought before it grabs hold of me. I have no time for indulgence. The coin of self-pity is too expensive, and besides, I've already spent it.

I am out of my time zone and off my regular routine. I haven't eaten since noon but have no thought of food. Prowling around the hotel, studying people, I look for anything that seems abnormal. Whatever that is.

Tue June 4 9:15 pm

Someone in the back of the room watches the crowd, expressionless. He seems to have a holster bulge. Could be a plainclothes cop, hired security or something far worse. I bump into him; it's nothing. I scrutinize everyone, ride the elevator up and down, familiarize myself with the layout, locate the exits. With a small part of my mind, I am dismayed at how professionally I am going about this task.

But it's a big place, enormous, and there are hundreds of people. Most seem excited, gay, keyed-up. Even the hotel workers seem exuberant. If Dallas was any indication, Smith may very well be in the hotel if the operation is to occur tonight. What will happen if we run into each other? Gunfight at the O.K. corral? At least I'll have the advantage of surprise; Smith won't be looking for me.

The Man on the Grassy Knoll

Of course he will. Any mistake I have ever made is because I underestimated Mr. Smith.

Tue June 4 11:08 pm

I talk to more people, monitor the returns. The results are close, too close to call, but RFK appears to be leading by a slight margin. He will address his supporters and staff in the Embassy Room as soon as a winner is declared. The room is cavernous, with a curved ceiling and inelegant chandeliers. It reminds me of a well-appointed subway station. A podium is set up onstage at the far end. The room is crowded and getting more so. If there are any plainclothes cops on the floor, I can't spot them. In fact, I don't see any of L.A.'s finest at all. It's almost unbelievable.

Has no one learned anything?

I picture Smith looking down on all this, that wry, crooked smile on his face.

Looking down?

My eyes traverse the walls above me. A few balloons drift here and there, but there's no place for a sharpshooter.

If the air conditioning is on, it's ineffective. I'm sweating in my sports jacket, although outside it's pleasant and cool, probably in the high sixties. I drift through the throng, eyes darting everywhere. There are lots of signs being waved around, obscuring visibility. One reporter estimates the crowd at about eighteen hundred people, an enormous number for a single room. Another tells me a press conference in the Colonial Room will follow Kennedy's address. I quickly locate the Colonial Room about forty yards away. That means Kennedy will probably work his way through the crowd on the floor and head down the hall to talk to the reporters. If

233

anything is to happen in Los Angeles, the hall seems the best opportunity. That's what I would do, I think. But the whole place is chaotic, and getting more so.

Tue June 4 11:45 pm

Rumors flash through the crowd: Kennedy is declaring victory. He has apparently eked out a close win. Someone says the television calls it 46% to 42%, with almost all precinct reporting. He'll be giving his speech in a few minutes. I work my way through the throng towards the podium. It's so crowded now it's difficult to move freely, and it's even hotter, if that's possible. I scan the crowd. No one looks suspicious, everyone looks suspicious. I have a helpless feeling.

Somewhere near, a man holds up a portable radio. The commentator reports the results, saying the delegate count now stands like this:

Hubert Humphrey   561
Robert F. Kennedy   393
Eugene McCarthy   258

Another reporter says that despite Kennedy's two victories this day, the consensus is that he is not going to win the Democratic nomination for President of the United States. Despite RFK's enormous popularity with the voters, Humphrey has the inside track on the delegates and this is supposed to be his year. I desperately hope so. I hope Mr. Smith thinks so.

Bobby Kennedy enters stage right, squeezing through the crowd on the podium, to roars of applause and sign-waving. Microphones and cameras are everywhere. The man is much smaller than I had imagined, almost elfin; the effect is magnified by the size of his bodyguards Rosey Grier and Rafer

The Man on the Grassy Knoll

Johnson. His wife Ethel is just behind him. Powerful lights illuminate the podium, driving the temperature up even further. The room is stifling. Kennedy flashes the victory sign several times and begins to talk. Signs wave; cheers erupt from time to time. He thanks everyone, including his dog. He goes on and on; it seems like forever. I'm not far from the podium, eyes darting here and there. I have to shade my eyes from the glare of the white-hot lights, which seem bright as suns. My hand goes to the Nagant as a nearby man in a rumpled suit reaches inside his jacket pocket. He comes out with a pen; he must be a reporter.

Finally, RFK waves, raises the victory sign a last time.

"Now it's on to Chicago, and let's win there." He flashes the famous Kennedy grin, runs his hand through his tousled hair, steps back. Some in the crowd begin to chant "We want Bobby." He turns to his right. It's difficult to see, but from my vantage point it appears someone is speaking in his ear. Now Kennedy turns to his left and heads to the rear. There must be a door there; I can't see.

But he's not coming through the crowd. He's not coming through the crowd.

Something's changed, or I got wrong information. Smith's words echo in my head: *All these guys use back stairways, freight entrances, employee entrances, kitchens, to get in and out. Those are can't miss opportunities . . .*

I feel a jolt of adrenaline. I push towards the stage, but it takes forever. Time has slowed down. I'm almost there. I am there.

I brace myself to hop up on the platform as I try to peer backstage. The crowd is in the way; I see nothing.

The Man on the Grassy Knoll

Wed June 5 12:15 am

Faintly, I hear what sounds like automatic weapons fire: rapid, many shots. Now there is screaming, yelling, pandemonium. Time accelerates madly.

I stop, horror-stricken. I am too late.

Part III

AFTERMATH

Chapter 36

At 12:15 on the morning of June 5, 1968, in a kitchen hallway at the Ambassador Hotel in Los Angeles, a Palestinian immigrant named Sirhan Sirhan emptied a cheap .22 Iver Johnson revolver at his target. Senator Robert F. Kennedy was hit three times, with a fourth bullet lodging in his suit jacket shoulder pad. Five others were wounded.

I knew, of course, Smith had utilized a second shooter, if for no other reason than the Iver Johnson held only eight rounds. As I struggled to follow Kennedy offstage, I had heard a fusillade of shots that could only have come from either a single automatic weapon or two guns in unison.

The similarities between Sirhan Sirhan and Lee Harvey Oswald were striking: both locals, both malcontents, working menial jobs, poorly educated, fringe members of society, defective personalities with inferior weapons. Both had spent considerable time in unfriendly nations. I guess the formula was tried and true, if incredibly obvious. I expected a firestorm of outrage, multiple investigations, perhaps another prestigious but empty committee. In reality, though, reaction was curiously muted. I didn't understand it. Smith had been the architect of both assassinations, utilizing the same methodology each time, almost to the last detail. How could this be? How could he get away with it?

The Man on the Grassy Knoll

Maybe the country had had enough; maybe we looked at ourselves and turned away. Mr. Smith was, in the end, a consummate judge of character. He had judged me, unerringly; he had correctly evaluated Oswald; he had accurately assessed an entire nation.

As time went by, and more sophisticated tools for analysis became available, it became evident there were serious problems with the single shooter theory in that kitchen hallway, just as there had been in Dealey Plaza. Using advanced forensic techniques, a 2008 study analyzing the only audio tape of the shooting concluded thirteen shots were fired, and perhaps more. How eerily redundant to the motorcycle cop's stuck microphone on Elm Street in Dallas, I thought. The report said several shots were too close together to have been fired consecutively from the same pistol. Just as I had recalled, it almost sounded like automatic weapons fire. Evidence presented at the 2008 American Academy of Forensic Sciences annual meeting in Washington, D.C. concluded there were two distinct acoustic signatures, indicating guns pointed in different directions. Witnesses placed the kitchen helper in front of Kennedy, but the coroner concluded there was no doubt the fatal shot came from behind the Senator's right ear, from a distance of approximately one inch.

Most interesting to me, two or three attendees at the Ambassador on the night of the shooting were identified from still pictures as senior CIA officers who worked together at JMWAVE, the anti-Castro station based in Miami that had housed Operation Mongoose.

It had been old home week in Los Angeles, I suppose.

Chapter 37

Perhaps one of the saddest and strangest aspects of the Dealey Plaza assassination was the willingness of a majority of the American people to believe Lee Harvey Oswald killed President Kennedy alone and without assistance. While there had been a vocal minority, some thoughtful and some deranged, I think most Americans wanted to believe justice had been done with the disposal of Oswald and that a conspiracy against a United States President was really unthinkable. The thought that a participant in the assassination was not caught is very disturbing. The national perception changed on March 6, 1975 when Geraldo Rivera showed the complete Zapruder film on his Goodnight America show.

I had little interest in the theories and speculation immediately following the events of November, 1963. I was trying to put Dallas behind me, especially during the difficult months that followed, when I was overcome with remorse and seeking to regain a semblance of stability. I did note that three spent cartridge casings were found by Ozzy's sixth floor window, confirming my impression at the time that Hidell/Oswald had gotten off a third round, simultaneously with mine. Subsequently, I maintained an interest in the Zapruder film because I knew evidence of a second shooter would have been recorded in that sequence, and the movie had the potential to cause serious problems. I dreaded seeing the film, but eventually I knew I would need to analyze it. As time passed, and the Warren Commission confirmed a simple version of the assassination, I began to wonder if perhaps Hidell did hit President Kennedy with his third and final shot. After all, the entire Warren Commission said so. How could that be? Certainly Smith or his people could not control that august body. So what did they see in the film? Did we both hit him? My mind began to form endless questions. Did Ozzy miss? Could I begin to hope, unlikely as it seemed, that Kennedy was already dead when my bullet slammed into him, a fraction of a second after Hidell's last shot? Or could I possibly have missed? Was I hallucinating? At the time, I was certain I had hit the target dead on, especially from such short range, but since everyone was buying Oswald's third shot I wanted further confirmation.

When the final frames of the Zapruder film were released to the public, gruesome as they were, it was clear the fatal shot blew the President's head violently backwards and to the left, apparently confirming what I really knew to be true. The debris from the impact went flying behind him. The resultant public uproar initiated further investigations. These inquiries concluded a second shooter was involved.

Yet I went a step further. I needed to be completely sure. Subsequently, another enhanced version of Zapruder was produced using advanced technology. Eventually, I obtained a video copy of this improved film. Part of this video focused on, and enlarged, the two limousine seats occupied by the Kennedys. I then observed the sequence on a very large screen television.

Using single-frame advance and stop action, I ran and reran the tape dozens and dozens of times, concentrating on

241

various areas of the screen. It was advantageous knowing the approximate actual sequence and timing of the shots from memory - as Hidell's firing was not unexpected the sequence was clear in my mind. Between that knowledge and running the film so many times I pieced together what I believe occurred in Dealey Plaza that day.

Oswald's first shot missed. Connally began to turn, perhaps to look toward the sound of the gunfire. The second bullet, fired just two seconds or so after the first round, hit both President Kennedy and Governor Connally. This is consistent with the Warren Commission findings. It seems clear that the President just began to react as he emerged from behind the sign in the Zapruder film. Connally reacted a split second later. The limousine drew closer to Zapruder and my position. The President slumped and leaned toward his wife, arms raised in reaction to the throat wound. That is about when I acquired him in my scope, beyond the retaining wall. I did not see Governor Connally or anyone else at the time.

Frame 313 recorded the fatal impact and the backsplash from the frontal shot. I then froze each separate frame and examined the film split second by split second, using single-frame advance. Eventually, I believe I found what I was looking for. Several frames later, while Kennedy's head recoiled from the impact, a single image shows the rear of the President's head distorted as a large fragment of skull seems to have been blown out the back, onto the limousine's rear deck behind Mrs. Kennedy. This is difficult to see for two reasons. First, Zapruder was not that far away from me. His camera angle was within ninety degrees of the shot trajectory, and the fragment was thus hidden from sight by the President's head until it reappeared, sliding backward along the trunk toward the left rear bumper, due to the forward motion of the limousine. It appears that Mrs. Kennedy retrieved the fragment just as Secret Service Agent Clint Hill mounted the limousine bumper.

Secondly, the single frame seems to show the piece just as it began to separate, but the picture is not totally clear as the dark shadow from the edged grass line beyond the limousine obscures this part of the frame. Then Zapruder jiggled the camera. It took many run-throughs on the very large screen to understand what I was seeing.

An imaginary line from the frontal impact point through the exit site on the rear deck traces backward toward the picket fence shooting area.

There is further evidence the fatal shot came from the front. Upon impact, the front of Kennedy's head was splayed open. There is a lag of several frames before the skull fragment was driven out the rear, as the hollow point bullet exploded following entry. This timing sequence would not seem possible with a jacketed bullet from the rear.

Finally, President Kennedy's hair provided further evidence for my analysis. Prior to the final bullet, Kennedy's hair could be seen laying neatly, despite the open convertible. The terrific force of the hollow point 7.62mm round literally exploded inside his head, and his hair mirrored the rearward effects of this massive detonation. Just before Mrs. Kennedy shoved the slain President's head below the level of the back seat, Kennedy's hair can be seen standing away from his head, showing the direction of the impact, acting as visible lines of force. It appears the entire rear of his head has been distorted backward, blown out from the fatal shot. Mrs. Kennedy appeared to react in horror at the damage to the back of the President's skull, rather than the front.

The character of the final, deadly shot seems consistent with a hollow point cartridge entering from the front, showing the devastating effect of a 7.62mm fully powered round, both at entry and exit, and appears uncharacteristic of a copper jacketed 6.5 bullet from the rear, as concluded by official inquiry.

To me, the evidence was overwhelming, though I wished with all my heart and soul I could believe otherwise.

It is logical to conclude the "magic bullet", the minimally distorted bullet, was likely Hidell's first shot, which hit no one. This becomes a more reasonable assumption when one does not have to account for just three shots, since there were really four. The bullet wounding Kennedy and Connally was almost certainly severely deformed and not recovered. It is illogical to think the "magic bullet" defied the laws of physics, emerging almost unscathed if it was the one wounding both men.

I emphasize that the above observations come primarily from viewing the film, as anyone can (albeit exhaustively), and only secondarily from the direct recollection of my view through the four power Tokarev scope. I am not a film technician, or a scientist, but I do have a unique basis for judging what the film shows. I am not positive but reasonably confident in these conclusions.

I have wished I could have had some expert assistance, but obviously this was not possible. I have also wished, through some miracle of miracles, I had missed and it was Hidell whose bullet found its fatal mark. But wishing does not

The Man on the Grassy Knoll

make it so, and all my tears have not washed out one frame of that nightmare film.

While I have confirmed, unfortunately, that my shot was the fatal one, it was possible that Hidell also hit the President in the head at about the same time. Perhaps that was the pristine bullet, hitting only soft tissue a fraction after the skull shattered, falling nearby. More likely, though, Hidell simply missed again with his crude weapon. By that time, his target was considerably farther away.

Although my analysis of the Zapruder film was as thorough and exhaustive as I could possibly perform, even a cursory examination clearly shows the President's head being slammed violently to the left rear. Strained and inconceivable explanations involving reflex actions, etc., have attempted to convince the citizenry they did not see what they have clearly seen - the shot really had to come from the right front. I suppose from my personal vantage point, seeing undeniable proof on film of my participation which is in fact denied, is fortunate. But the Emperor's New Clothes syndrome proves we believe what we want to believe, even when we see otherwise.

Mr. Smith must have known this all along; doubtless it is this human frailty that allows work like his to continue without resistance, without accountability, without fetters. The frightening events of 1962 and 1963 within the Kennedy administration and the top levels of the clandestine services bear this out with shuddering clarity. I wonder if Smith was telling me more than I realized when he asked me if I had read *Johnny Got His Gun.* A long while later, I recalled the book's last sentence: "You plan the wars you masters of men plan the wars and point the way and we will point the gun." Mr. Smith pointed the way and I pointed the gun. Sadly, I think this will always be the way of us. Mr. Smith, and those like him, all believe they work for Good - no one but madmen believe they work for Evil. The axiom is that the ends justify the means. What I have tragically learned, at great cost, is that there are no ends, only means.

Chapter 38

And so I reflect back on my participation, on my actions those years ago, two lifetimes ago, unable to lay it all to rest, unable to quantify, measure, fold away. I sift and prod, this tortured jigsaw puzzle that has been my existence, trying to put the pieces together on a crooked, ill-made table, the odds and ends of my life, pieces that won't dovetail, no coherent picture on the box to guide me. In the end I have only small sections, fragments, only a hint of what they form, what they mean. I began this journal by saying I do not think you will weep for me.

I think I am not such a good actor. I think that as we concluded our meeting in Las Vegas, Mr. Smith realized I was not able to perform his infernal task. I believe that, above all, he was a consummate judge of character, and that he saw through my eyes into the agony of my soul. And he moved on.

I turn over the events of 1963, sift and measure, because that was the only time I had a choice. Mr. Smith had tried to give me absolution, when we met again in 1968, detailing for me the inevitability of our actions in Dallas. In the end, I believe most of what he told me, but I don't know if it is enough.

*   *   *

The Man on the Grassy Knoll

But I do know the missiles had really been there, ready to go after all, controlled by Cuban forces, without restraint from the Soviet Union. That hadn't been contrived, it was true enough: not just part of the story to convince me. How do you convince someone, even an impressionable, small town kid just out of school, to whack the President of the United States, even after he had made the leap to go from a normal, unremarkably solid life to an operation against an acknowledged enemy in Cuba? How do you do that? You have to show him things, the high technology trappings of the spy trade, all official and important, seemingly hard intelligence data gathered by the military, tell him elaborate stories, make it appear as if all the senior members of the intelligence community and the whole government are behind the operation, behind him. You have to tell him he's the only one for the job, at least at the moment, and the moment is critical. You have to convince him the Kennedys have gone over the top, run amok, and are threatening the existence of his loved ones in a potpourri of fireballs across America, a *Dr. Strangelove, Seven Days in May, The Manchurian Candidate* and *Fail-Safe* all rolled into one. You have to offer a fortune, not only as an inducement, but as a sign of solidarity behind the operation. You gain the trust of the youth, become as a father figure, and lead with authority. Smith had done all that, and in a short amount of time. In wartime, he would have extracted a confession out of me to parade on television screens across Vietnam, I suppose, and I probably would have believed I had done it. He was a magnetic force, and good at his job, and I had followed him like a lemming over the edge, like Patty Hearst with her weapon in that California bank, or maybe even like the Manson family. Perhaps our time in

248

The Man on the Grassy Knoll

Nassau and Miami was deliberately planned to drive the point home, to provide sensory input as to how near the shadowy threat was supposed to be, and how much beauty was at risk.

And despite the deception, Smith's artful duplicity, I knew and believed the unthinkable really could have happened. The cold war could have gone over the edge, because it almost had twice in two years. Those dangerous men from the President on down really had spun out of control, and the clashing of swords had occurred. Maybe Smith had saved the world, after all. I didn't really believe it, not completely, but maybe that was true and that meant that maybe I had done so too. Not like the Manson family or Patty Hearst, after all.

Maybe it depended if I thought about it in the dead of night or during the day, after a couple of beers or just a soda, alone on a beach at sunset or in a crowd at a ball game, because I was never going to know for sure. I do know I sought my own redemption as I crept into the bathroom of that resort hotel, and then again on the ballroom floor of another, the Ambassador, and failed both times.

I do not think redemption can come at the point of a gun.

And once in a while I unfold the note that came in the mail on November 22, 1973. The envelope had been addressed to John David M____, the identity I had assumed in 1968 when I went underground to escape retribution from Mr. Smith, when I disappeared without a trace – or so I thought - and launched my unsuccessful attempt to stop the assassination of Robert F. Kennedy. The envelope, with no return address but postmarked McLean, Virginia, had been sent unerringly to my home, and the unsigned message had stopped me cold.

249

The Man on the Grassy Knoll

John, I am sorry for having done what I did to your life. But in the end, I'm not sorry we did it. I'm just sorry we had to do it.

Just sorry we had to do it. That's what he said.

Chapter 39

In the beginning of this journal, or whatever it is, I mentioned two occurrences that could trigger publication of this work. At this point, most everyone else - perhaps everyone - is dead, and there is no real reason not to bring this all to light, this incredible, unknown chapter of American history.

It is finished.

*　　*　　*　　*　　*

I can see the beauty in the sunsets again, but I have never been back to Texas. I think about Mr. Smith, who doubted nothing, who had the confidence to relentlessly pursue his ends, and who believed in what our unholy trio had done. He would be old now, if he is still alive, old enough to think of the end of him, and I wonder where he is and if any of the nightmares plague him. Somehow, I don't think so.

*　　*　　*　　*　　*

It is now said: there was a man on the grassy knoll that fatal Friday at 12:30 p.m., a man with a Soviet 7.62mm sniper rifle who carried out his fierce errand under the tutelage of a small, powerful group, men who considered themselves patriots, who gave him reasons and money, both of which in the end were, on balance, found wanting.

The Man on the Grassy Knoll

Certainly, some who read this, when and if it sees the light of day, will label it fiction, fraud or fancy, whether from an analytical skepticism or an emotional need to do so. They miss the point. I truly wish it were. For me, the echoes in Dealey Plaza can never fade away. And louder than those echoes, louder than the gunshots that reverberated around Dealey Plaza, more deafening than the fusillade of shots that rang out from Ambassador Hotel pantry, louder than anything, the words of Mr. Smith reverberate still in my head:

Who's to stop us?

Who's to stop us?

- The End -

Appendix

Grassy knoll at instant of fatal shot.
Polaroid photo by Mary Moorman (public domain).

Tokarev SVT40 sniper rifle with PE scope

Contents of Safety Deposit Box

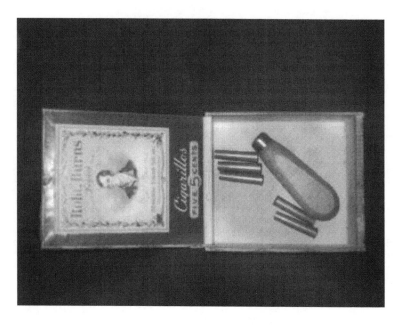

Cigar box with dedicated 7.62 Russian ammunition for Nagant pistol and tool handle.

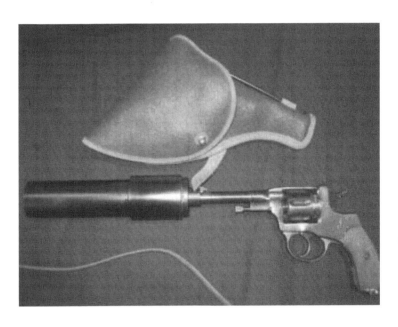

1931 Nagant pistol furnished by Mr. Smith, with holster and attached suppressor.

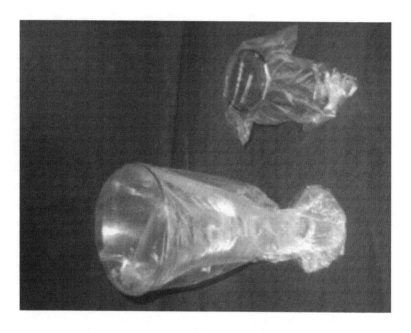

Glasses used by Mr. Smith, 1963, taken from restaurants on two occasions

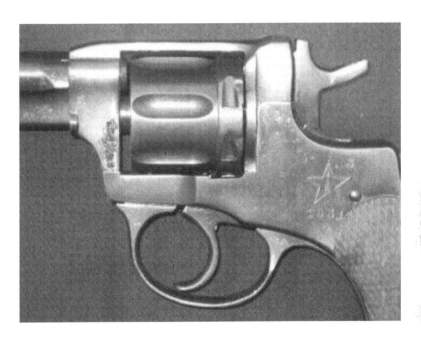

Nagant pistol, showing star and defaced serial number. Note
markings on trigger and trigger guard.

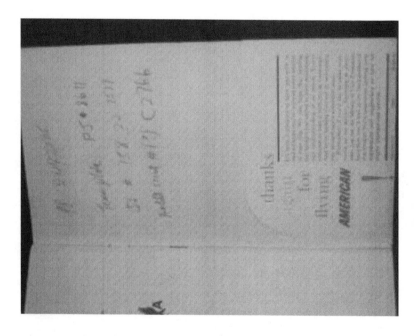

Inside back of ticket envelope from flight #55, Dallas-Los Angeles, Nov 22, 1963 with handwritten notes listing:

John Graves passport number D092505
Texas license plate number PJ*8611
John Graves social security number 158 22 7577
Hidell rifle serial number C2766

Ticket from flight #55, Dallas-Los Angeles, Nov 22, 1963 in Welcome Aboard pamphlet

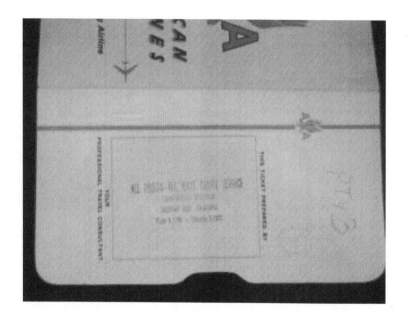

Back of ticket envelope from flight #55, Dallas-Los Angeles, Nov 22, 1963 indicating ticket supplier and bearing penciled note "PTY3"

American Airlines Welcome Aboard pamphlet from Flight #55, Dallas-Los Angeles Nov 22, 1963

11396626R0016

Made in the USA
Lexington, KY
30 September 2011